Artisan VEGAN CHEESE

FROM EVERYDAY TO GOURMET

Miyoko Schinner

Book Publishing Company
Summertown, Tennessee

Library of Congress Cataloging-in-Publication Data

Schinner, Miyoko Nishimoto, 1957-
    Artisan vegan cheese : from everyday to gourmet / Miyoko Schinner.
        p.   cm.
    Includes index.
    ISBN 978-1-57067-283-5 (pbk.) — ISBN 978-1-57067-927-8 (e-book)
  1. Vegan cooking.   2. Cheesemaking.   3. Cooking (Cheese)   4. Dairy-free diet.
I. Title.
    TX837.S289 2012
    641.6'73—dc23

                                                                2012012868

Cover and interior design: John Wincek

Photography by Lily Dong, lilydongphotography.com

Printed on recycled paper

Book Publishing Co. is a member of Green Press Initiative. We chose to print this title on paper with postconsumer recycled content, processed without chlorine, which saved the following natural resources:

63 trees
1,839 pounds of solid waste
29,025 gallons of wastewater
6,437 pounds of greenhouse gases
26 million BTU of total energy

For more information, visit greenpressinitiative.org.

Paper calculations from Environmental Defense Paper Calculator, edf.org/papercalculator.

Printed in the United States

Book Publishing Company
P.O. Box 99
Summertown, TN 38483
888-260-8458
bookpubco.com

ISBN 13: 978-1-57067-283-5

23 22 21 20 19 18   10 11 12 13 14 15

Calculations for the nutritional analyses in this book are based on the average number of servings listed with the recipes and the average amount of an ingredient if a range is called for. Calculations are rounded up to the nearest gram. If two options for an ingredient are listed, the first one is used. The analyses include oil used for frying. Not included are optional ingredients and serving suggestions.

Contents

Foreword

At long last we have a great alternative to dairy-based cheese for those who are lactose intolerant or who want a substitute for animal products for any of a number of reasons, including concerns about health because of the cholesterol and saturated fats in dairy products, about the environmental impacts of animal agriculture, or about the often cruel treatment of dairy animals. For many people transitioning to a plant-based diet, the most difficult type of food to give up is cheese. Miyoko Schinner can help you satisfy those cravings with the recipes in this book. Whether you favor sharp Cheddar or rich, creamy Brie, you'll find her recipes amazing, and vegans and nonvegans alike will be impressed when you serve these cheeses and dishes made with them. In fact, they may even accuse you of sneaking in some dairy products.

I can easily state that Miyoko is the most talented chef I have known. Over the past decade, she has been doing demos and workshops for groundbreaking physician and author John McDougall, MD, and for World Veg Festival, a celebration of World Vegetarian Day sponsored by San Francisco Vegetarian Society. All of her creations dazzle the taste buds, add pleasure to dining, and will satisfy even epicureans with the most elevated expectations.

In the past, Miyoko has shared her brilliance in her cookbooks *Japanese Cooking: Contemporary and Traditional* and *The New Now and Zen Epicure*, which offer a wonderful variety of delicious yet mostly straightforward dishes. Both are great resources for anyone seeking satisfying, healthful alternatives to the standard American diet.

Miyoko took a hiatus from her professional culinary endeavors for a few years to focus on her family, but now she's back, and we welcome her with open arms. Between this book and her television series, *Miyoko's Kitchen*, we can all once again enjoy her elegant and healthful creations.

Dixie Mahy
PRESIDENT, SAN FRANCISCO VEGETARIAN SOCIETY

Preface

My Year of Vegan Cheeses

I have been wanting to write this book for thirty years. That's not to say that I had a trove of vegan cheese recipes ready to be compiled into a book thirty years ago; back then they were just flickers of ideas floating around my mind. But I knew that one day I would develop some really credible vegan cheeses, and I kept promising people I'd do that. Well, this has been my year of vegan cheeses.

It started sometime in the spring of 2010. I had been intrigued for several years by the nut-based cheeses popular in the raw food community and had been playing around with them. The majority of vegan cheeses I had sampled were more like spreads, requiring a stretch of the imagination to think of them as cheese. But a few were stellar, notably the raw cheeses made by Roxanne Klein at her all-too-ephemeral restaurant, Roxanne's. Café Gratitude, a chain of vegan restaurants in the Bay Area, also had some winners on their menu. Still, if they were raw, they didn't melt. There was also, of course, the ever-increasing number of commercially available vegan cheeses that melted to a degree, which had improved in quality and variety over the years, but to my taste buds they still had a somewhat artificial flavor and weren't up to "cheese board standards." What to do?

The answer was clear. It was time to make good on my promise. With a vegetarian fundraiser at my house coming up, I decided to spend a few weeks experimenting with nut-based cheeses. My goal was to put together a platter of vegan cheeses as the centerpiece of the buffet. I figured that the vegan and vegetarian community would be supportive of any attempt at cheese, making this a safe venue in which to embark on my venture. I presented Brie, flavored chèvre, Gruyère, and a few other cheeses. And then I retreated to the kitchen to see how people reacted. Well, they raved. Afterward I even heard from people who hadn't been there but had found out about the cheeses through the grapevine. That was all great feedback, but hey, it was still a vegan crowd.

So I kept at it, coming up with more varieties, and I started serving them to my omnivorous friends, including at a big holiday party. Their reactions were the same as those from the vegans and vegetarians, only the omnivores often told me that they couldn't tell the difference between my cheeses and "the real stuff." This was exciting, and I threw myself headlong into my cheese experiment.

My kitchen became a laboratory, with cheeses lying around everywhere as I attempted to age them while fending off mold. People would look quizzically at the rounds strewn around the kitchen and wonder what they were. From the initial nut-based cheeses to varieties made from yogurt to the day I finally found a way to make a vegan cheese that actually melted, I had a couple of cheeses in the works at all times and would prod anyone who walked into the house into trying some. Some of the cheeses were, of course, less delectable, and a few ended up in my compost pile, but many met with rave reviews.

It has now been about a year since my big cheese experiment began, and I finally have that trove of cheese recipes. But the journey has only just begun. As the deadline for this book fast approaches, I continue to dream up new ways to make cheeses and another lightbulb turns on—and then I have to remind myself that now is the time for me to buckle down and finish writing this book rather than puttering around the kitchen. So for the time being, I don't have as many cheeses sitting on my counters, but I'll be back in my cheese laboratory soon enough, developing more recipes to add to the next edition of this book. In the meantime, I hope you'll find these cheeses fun and compelling enough to serve not only to vegans but to your omnivorous friends as well.

Who knows, perhaps this will be your year of vegan cheeses.

Acknowledgments

Over the years, many people encouraged me to delve into the subject of homemade vegan cheese, and to all of them I owe gratitude for their faith in me. Once I started the process, however, there is one young person to whom I am indebted—as unfair as this may seem—for providing the utterly simple insight about vegan cheeses in general. "They all taste somewhat tangy, as if they have lemon juice in them. Dairy cheese isn't tangy—it's sharp." This person is my youngest daughter, a teen with worldly tastes and an impeccable palate. She put me on track to pursue how to culture the cheese, not just add tangy flavorings to it. To you, Cammy, I dedicate this book!

Of course, I cannot neglect to thank my other family members who endured kitchen counters covered with cheese experiments, and night after night of cheesy dishes that made them wish for just a simple salad. My husband, Michael, who encouraged me and honestly critiqued each cheese I created; my oldest daughter, Sera, who hated vegan cheeses and suffered through my experiments but eventually grew to like them (and who now asks for vegan grilled cheese sandwiches); and my son, Aki, who upon returning home from college refused to believe that my Sun-Dried Tomato and Garlic Cream Cheese was really made from cashews—to all of them, I am grateful. Beyond my family were my friends—vegan, nonvegan, nonvegetarian—who willingly tasted and critiqued, but mostly raved, about my creations. Had it not been for their encouragement, I don't know if I would have believed in myself enough to move ahead. In particular, I would like to thank Maggie, a writer herself, who spent countless hours with me in conversation about the book, its style, and the angle of presentation.

While I pride myself in providing recipes that are for the most part original, like most chefs, I borrow ideas directly or indirectly from other chefs, cookbooks, and restaurants, often adapting them into my own creations. In this book, I want to give credit for the easy Almond Milk recipe (page 54) to Chef AJ, who demonstrated the shortcut method in one of her fun videos.

When it came time to send the manuscript to the publisher, I truly felt it was in pretty good shape. But reality hit as soon as my editor, Jo Stepaniak, of cookbook fame herself, sent back some pages to me completely marked up. There were grueling weeks ahead, with rewriting and proofreading my book again and again, and still, as we approach the end of this process, Jo sends me queries about recipes that get me reeling—but upon yet another review of my own recipes, I think to myself, "How could I have left that out?" This is why we shouldn't try to proofread and edit completely on our own—a good pair of eyes belonging to a professional editor is so important! So thank you, Jo, for what felt like beatings and lashings but were ever so necessary. Finally, I'd like to thank Bob and Cynthia at Book Publishing Company, who believed in me enough to give me the green light on my first book in over a decade.

And to you, dear reader, thank you!

Introduction

If you like instant gratification, you've picked up the wrong book. My intention in saying that isn't to scare you away, but to inform you that making the cheeses in this book will require your patience and love—not as much patience as may be required for making a dairy cheese, which often takes months, but enough that you'll usually have to wait a few days or more to taste your creations. Rest assured, however, that the amount of work involved in making each cheese is but a few minutes . . . and then you just have to wait. Your patience will be rewarded. After all, as they say, wine, cheese— and even some of us—improve with age.

Cultured Flavor

It was my youngest daughter who remarked, when eating one of my earlier attempts at vegan cheese, that it was more *tangy* than *sharp*. That got me thinking about the difference between vegan cheeses and dairy cheese. What transforms simple milk into cheese is a culturing process that begins with various bacteria and enzymes, which coagulate the proteins in the milk, allowing the solids to separate from the whey. The cheese is then aged for a few days to many months, and during that time it develops its distinctive character and flavor. Depending on the type of enzymes and bacteria used, as well as certain molds for bloomy-rind and blue-veined cheeses, the final product takes on different characteristics.

With vegan cheeses, the process is a little different. The proteins in soy milk and nut milks react differently to culturing agents and don't tend to coagulate in such a way that curds separate out, and therefore must be processed and aged using somewhat different methods. Therefore, most vegan cheeses on the market today aren't cultured or aged; instead, they're made to taste like cheese through the addition of flavorings, often utilizing an acidic ingredient, such as lemon juice, to imitate a sharp flavor. As my daughter's remark indicated, this often results in more of a tanginess than a sharpness.

1

What makes the cheeses in this book different is that they gain their cheeselike qualities from culturing and varying degrees of aging, rather than the addition of acidic ingredients. This helps create not only sharpness but also more flavor, depth, and umami—that extremely satisfying savory taste designated as the fifth basic flavor. Achieving this complexity of flavor is something you simply cannot rush—you must let the process unfold naturally. Of course, you will have to monitor it, as ambient temperature, humidity, and other conditions can affect how quickly cheeses culture, age, or spoil. But the reward for your patience and love are fabulous cheeses that can be used just like their dairy counterparts in myriad culinary applications. With these cheeses, you will be able to create vegan versions of some of your favorite recipes that incorporate cheese—something you may have thought impossible.

Once you make these cheeses, you can store them in your refrigerator (and in most cases in your freezer) so you'll have them on hand whenever you want to cock with them. If you're a longtime vegan and have forgotten how to cook with cheese, chapters 7 through 9 offer delectable appetizers, entrées, and desserts made with the recipes for cheeses and other dairy alternatives in the earlier chapters of this book.

Even if you still balk at making anything that takes more than a few minutes. you're still in luck. Chapter 4 is devoted to recipes for almost-instant cheeses that are pretty tasty as well.

A Snapshot of the Cheese-Making Process

Here's a glimpse of what you'll find in "Miyoko's Cheese Shop" and what you ll need to set up a cheese shop of your own. This section will give you an idea of what to expect and what tools and ingredients you'll need in order for your cheese-making endeavors to be successful.

First of all, you'll need a culturing agent. For most of the cheeses in this book, that will be some form of probiotic—a substance that contains friendly bacteria that help turn the base ingredient into cheese, or at least contribute to the flavor. While powdered probiotics can accomplish this, these products tend to be very expensive, and often they aren't vegan. Their strength also differs from brand to brand, so I've chosen not to use them in this book, although you can certainly experiment with them if you wish. Instead, these cheeses are primarily cultured with rejuvelac or nondairy yogurt.

Rejuvelac, a fermented beverage made from whole grains, contains a variety of friendly bacteria, including some that produce lactic acid, which contributes to sharpness. It can easily be made at home using widely available whole grains, such as brown rice or rye, spelt, or wheat berries. Although you can probably buy rejuvelac at your local natural food store, I recommend that you make it as the first step on your journey into vegan cheeses. Also note that store-bought rejuvelac is generally made with sprouted wheat berries, so if you are intolerant to wheat, you'll want to make your own using another whole grain. The recipe for making your own rejuvelac (page 6) is simple, but it does take several days. Whether homemade or store-bought, rejuvelac works beautifully as a culturing agent.

Nondairy yogurt, which is also used as a culture for many of the cheeses in this book, is widely available commercially. However, if you save a little store-bought yogurt, you can use that to make your own yogurt (page 56).

The base ingredients of the cheeses range from nuts to soy milk to soy yogurt. Many of the cheeses utilize methods developed by raw foodists and involve culturing puréed cashews or other nuts, although with my own spin to them, which in some cases result in a product that isn't raw. While nuts make great cheeses, those cheeses don't melt because the base is a solid substance that cannot get any softer. In order to make cheeses that melt, I took a cue from dairy cheeses and experimented with using nondairy yogurt as the base, because it's more liquid, and then adding oil. The majority of the cheeses in this book, however, do not contain oil.

Traditionally, hard cheeses are made by pressing as much whey out of the curds as possible, leaving behind largely solidified protein and fat. Although some recipes for raw nut-based cheeses call for putting the cheese in a colander and pressing it by weighting the top with river rocks, bricks, or other heavy objects, I find it difficult to get consistent results with this method. If you want to make cheeses that are hard or just firmer, a cheese press is invaluable—and you'll also need much more time and patience.

Furthermore, because many of the cheeses in this book don't involve separating curds from liquid ingredients analogous to whey, I opted for an easier method of firming up the hard cheeses (semifirm, really): adding natural thickening agents such as agar, carrageenan, tapioca flour, and xanthan gum. You may be able to find these at your grocery store, but I've also provided information on online suppliers (see page 137). Carrageenan yields a better texture than agar, but agar can be used in almost every recipe in this book except the meltable cheeses in chapter 3. Note that when substituting agar powder for carrageenan powder, you'll need to double the amount.

Adding thickening agents has its drawbacks, however. If too much is used, the texture of the cheese becomes somewhat gelatinous. Consequently, the "hard" cheeses in this book are somewhat softer than dairy cheeses. In chapter 2, you'll find air-dried cheeses, which develop a harder texture as they dry. This can take from several days to several weeks, depending on the variety; for example, Air-Dried Parmesan (page 34), which is quite hard, dries for two to three weeks.

You probably already have most of the equipment you'll need, and if not, it can be purchased at a kitchen supply store. You'll need a blender, preferably a high-speed model. A regular blender will also work; just be sure that when making nut-based cheeses you soak the nuts for the longer amount of time indicated in the recipe. I find that food processors generally don't purée nuts as well as blenders do, although this may depend on the brand and model. You will also need molds for shaping many of the cheeses (see sidebar, page 4). For air-dried cheeses, you'll need a wire rack like those used for cooling baked goods. Other helpful tools are cheesecloth, a colander, a food processor, parch-

In many cases, the cheeses in this book are shaped in a mold. There are no strict rules about what sort of mold to use, other than using a glass or nonreactive metal container. You don't need to go out and buy any special molds; you can probably make use of things you already have in your kitchen. Small loaf pans, ramekins, bowls, storage containers, and cake pans are all great options.

When deciding what type of mold to use, consider the type of cheese you're making and what size you want the finished cheese to be. For the Sharp Cheddar (page 14), you might opt to use just one loaf pan to make a large block of cheese, while for Cashew Chèvre (page 8), you might choose to use several ramekins. Or you can toss tradition to the wind and make small, round Cheddar cheeses and square blocks of chèvre!

While most of the cheeses will come right out of the mold once firm, you may want to line the mold with cheesecloth or plastic wrap for easier removal.

ment paper, wooden spoons, whisks, a heavy medium-sized saucepan, and a sieve. For making yogurt, farmer's cheese, and deep-fried foods, a kitchen thermometer is very handy. For many of the desserts in chapter 9, you'll need a springform pan and an electric mixer. That's about it for equipment!

The Proof Is in the Cheese

The idea behind most of my cheese recipes is that you can use the cheeses to replace their dairy counterparts in every way, including in almost any recipe that calls for cheese. You can store them as long in your refrigerator—and some of them just keep getting better with time. So read on and make several of the cheeses in chapters 1 through 4. Although it may seem daunting at first, they're really quite easy to make. Once you have them on hand in your fridge, you can pull out some old cookbooks, dust them off, and replicate old favorite recipes that called for cheese. Maybe you'll be craving a grilled cheese sandwich, or perhaps you'll want to put together an amazing cheese plate for a party. Either way, all you'll need to do is go to your refrigerator.

Make sure that the salt you use to process the cheese and coat the outside for air-drying is noniodized. Iodized salt can kill or retard lactic acid cultures, leading to mold growth and unsuccessful culturing.

1

Artisan and Aged Cheeses

In this age of instant gratification, few people are willing to embrace time-honored traditions such as making wine and cheese. But because you're reading this book, I will assume you are one of those patient souls willing to wait for something special. Brie, Cheddar, fresh mozzarella, Gruyère—these are but a few of the rewards that await you in this first chapter. Yes, you'll have to bide your time during the process, but don't wait now to get started!

An easily made fermented beverage filled with probiotics and lactic acid, rejuvelac is the primary culturing agent for many of the cheeses in this book. Because it will keep for two to three weeks in the refrigerator, it's a good idea to always have some on hand so you can get a head start on cheese making. Depending on the temperature in your house, you'll need to allow four to seven days for the rejuvelac to be fully cultured. Rejuvelac is also available commercially at many natural food stores.

REJUVELAC

MAKES ABOUT 5 CUPS

1 cup whole grains (such as brown rice, Kamut berries, millet, oat groats, quinoa, rye berries, wheat berries, or a combination)

6 cups filtered water

1. **Soak and sprout the grains.**

   Put the grains in a 1-quart glass jar and add water to cover. Place a double layer of cheesecloth over the mouth of the jar and secure it with a rubber band. Let the grains soak for 8 to 12 hours. Drain, then add just enough water to moisten the grains but not so much that they are immersed in water. Put the jar in a warm place out of direct sunlight for 1 to 3 days and rinse the grains once or twice a day, each time draining well and then adding just enough fresh water to moisten them. Continue this process until the grains have begun to sprout (they will have little tails emerging).

2. **Culture the rejuvelac.**

   Divide the sprouted grains equally between two 1-quart glass jars. Pour 3 cups of the filtered water into each jar. Cover each jar with fresh cheesecloth and secure it with rubber bands. Put the jars in a warm place out of direct sunlight for 1 to 3 days. The water will turn cloudy and white, and the liquid will have a slightly tart flavor, somewhat like lemon juice. Strain the liquid into clean glass jars and discard the grains.

   STORAGE NOTES: Covered and stored in the refrigerator, Rejuvelac will keep for about 4 weeks.

   NOTE: Make sure the grains you are using are not pre-sprouted. Quinoa is one of the fastest and easiest grains to use for this recipe, as it often sprouts in less than a day (depending on the ambient temperature).

Although delicious in its own right, this simple recipe also serves as the basis for many of the other cheeses in this chapter. Depending on how you plan to use it and how mild or sharp you want the cheese to be, you can shorten or lengthen the culturing time. The cheese will continue to culture in the refrigerator, getting stronger and sharper in flavor.

basic CASHEW CHEESE

MAKES ABOUT 1 POUND

2 cups raw cashews, soaked in water for 3 to 8 hours and drained

Pinch salt

¼ to ½ cup rejuvelac (preferably homemade, page 6)

Per ounce: calories: 105, protein: 3 g, fat: 8 g, saturated fat: 1 g, carbohydrate: 5 g, sodium: 3 mg, calcium: 7 mg

1. **Process the ingredients.**

Put the cashews and salt in a blender. Turn on the blender and pour in just enough of the rejuvelac through the cap opening in the lid to process the cashews. (The longer the cashews have soaked, the less liquid will be required for processing. Also note that a high-powered blender can process the cashews with less added liquid.) Process until smooth and creamy, occasionally stopping to scrape down the blender jar and move the mixture toward the blades.

2. **Culture the cheese.**

Transfer to a clean glass bowl or container, cover, and let rest at room temperature for 8 to 36 hours, depending on how sharp a flavor you want and the ambient temperature (culturing will proceed more quickly at warmer temperatures). The cheese will thicken as it cultures.

3. **Form the cheese.**

If you will eventually be using the cheese as a base for another recipe, simply cover and store it in the refrigerator for up to 2 weeks. Otherwise, transfer to a glass or nonreactive metal mold and smooth the top. Cover and refrigerate for at least 6 hours, until firm.

STORAGE NOTES: Wrapped in plastic wrap and stored in a ziplock bag in the refrigerator, Basic Cashew Cheese will keep for about 2 weeks. It can be stored longer, but it will continue to get sharper and stronger in flavor, so taste it occasionally. Once it has achieved the desired flavor, it can be stored in the freezer for up to 4 months.

NOTE: Several other recipes use Basic Cashew Cheese as a foundation. These recipes require the cheese to have various degrees of sharpness. Be sure to read other such recipes in advance so you'll know how long to culture the Basic Cashew Cheese to achieve the necessary sharpness.

With just a tweak to the Basic Cashew Cheese, you can create a cheese akin to soft goat cheese, or chèvre. Actual goat's milk cheese varies in the degree of sharpness, and you can achieve the same sort of variation in the amount of "edge" by varying the culturing time. For a mild cheese, culture for just a day; for a sharper one, two to three days. Try this cheese stuffed in fresh figs, tossed in a salad with pears and walnuts, or spread on crackers.

cashew CHÈVRE

MAKES ABOUT 1 POUND

1 pound Basic Cashew Cheese
(page 7), **cultured for 1 to 3 days**

1 tablespoon nutritional yeast flakes

½ teaspoon salt

1. **Flavor the cheese.**
   Put the Basic Cashew Cheese, nutritional yeast, and salt in a large bowl. Mix well.

2. **Form the cheese.**
   Line a glass or nonreactive metal mold with cheesecloth or plastic wrap. Pack in the cheese and smooth the top. Cover and refrigerate for at least 6 hours, until firm. When ready to serve, use the cheese-cloth or plastic wrap to help unmold the cheese.

STORAGE NOTES: Wrapped in plastic wrap and stored in a ziplock bag in the refrigerator, Cashew Chèvre will keep for up to 2 weeks. It can be stored longer, but it will continue to get sharper and stronger in flavor, so taste it occasionally. Once it has achieved the desired flavor, it can be stored in the freezer for up to 4 months.

HERBED CHÈVRE ROLL: Shape the cheese into one large log or two or three smaller logs. Roll in ¾ cup minced fresh herbs, such as basil, parsley, sage, tarragon, thyme, or a combination.

LEMON-GARLIC CHÈVRE: Add the grated zest of 1 lemon and 2 to 3 cloves of garlic, minced, along with the nutritional yeast and salt.

Per ounce: calories: 106, protein: 4 g, fat: 8 g, saturated fat: 1 g, carbohydrate: 5 g, sodium: 69 mg, calcium: 7 mg

This cheese is similar to Cashew Chèvre (page 8), but it's dressed up with fragrant lemon zest and peppercorns, transforming it into an artisan cheese of the finest quality. Serve it with sliced pears or apples, a baguette, and chilled Pinot Grigio. It also makes a great gift during the winter holidays.

CASHEW CHÈVRE with lemon zest and peppercorns

MAKES ABOUT 12 OUNCES

1½ cups Basic Cashew Cheese
(page 7), cultured for 1 to 2 days
(see note)

Grated zest of 1 lemon

2 tablespoons freshly squeezed
lemon juice

1 tablespoon nutritional yeast flakes

½ teaspoon salt

2 to 3 tablespoons whole black or
multicolored peppercorns

1. **Flavor the cheese.**
   Put the Basic Cashew Cheese, lemon zest and juice, nutritional yeast, and salt in a large bowl. Mix well.

2. **Form the cheese.**
   Line a small cake pan or similar-sized glass or nonreactive metal mold with cheesecloth or plastic wrap. Sprinkle the peppercorns evenly in the pan, using enough to mostly cover the bottom of the pan. Pack in the cheese and smooth the top. Cover and refrigerate for at least 6 hours, until firm. When ready to serve, use the cheesecloth or plastic wrap to help unmold the cheese.

STORAGE NOTES: Wrapped in plastic wrap and stored in a ziplock bag in the refrigerator, Cashew Chèvre with Lemon Zest and Peppercorns will keep for about 2 weeks. It can be stored longer, but it will continue to get sharper and stronger in flavor. Once it has achieved the desired flavor, it can be stored in the freezer for up to 4 months.

VARIATION: Substitute Creamy Yogurt Cheese (page 23) for the Basic Cashew Cheese.

NOTE: This recipe will turn out best if you don't let the Basic Cashew Cheese get too tangy.

Per ounce: calories: 108, protein: 4 g, fat: 8 g, saturated fat: 1 g, carbohydrate: 6 g, sodium: 92 mg, calcium: 8 mg

This soft and aromatic cheese redolent of herbs and garlic makes a beautiful centerpiece for any cheese platter. If there's any left over, use it the next day as a delicious sandwich filling with roasted vegetables. Although the herbs in this recipe emulate the flavor of classic Boursin, other herbs, such as basil, oregano, parsley, and rosemary, can be substituted.

BOURSIN

See photo facing page 23.

MAKES ABOUT 1 POUND

1 pound Basic Cashew Cheese (page 7), cultured for 1 to 2 days (see note)

¼ cup minced fresh parsley

2 tablespoons nutritional yeast flakes

2 to 3 cloves garlic, minced

1 tablespoon minced fresh chervil, or 1 teaspoon dried

1 tablespoon minced fresh tarragon, or 1 teaspoon dried

2 teaspoons minced fresh thyme, or ¾ teaspoon dried

1 teaspoon salt

½ teaspoon dried marjoram

1. **Flavor the cheese.**

Put the Basic Cashew Cheese, parsley, nutritional yeast, 2 cloves of the garlic, and the chervil, tarragon, thyme, salt, and marjoram in a large bowl. Mix well. Taste and add more garlic if desired.

2. **Form the cheese.**

The cheese can be shaped in a mold or be formed into a log or ball by hand. To use a mold, line it with cheesecloth or plastic wrap, pack in the cheese, and smooth the top. Cover or wrap well with plastic wrap and refrigerate for at least 6 hours, until firm.

STORAGE NOTES: Wrapped in plastic wrap and stored in a ziplock bag in the refrigerator, Boursin will keep for about 2 weeks. It can be stored longer, but it will continue to get sharper and stronger in flavor, so taste it occasionally. Once it has achieved the desired flavor, it can be stored in the freezer up to 4 months.

VARIATION: Substitute Creamy Yogurt Cheese (page 23) for the Basic Cashew Cheese.

NOTE: This recipe will turn out best if you don't let the Basic Cashew Cheese get too tangy.

Per ounce: calories: 109, protein: 4 g, fat: 8 g, saturated fat: 2 g, carbohydrate: 6 g, sodium: 137 mg, calcium: 10 mg

Here's a fun way to flavor Basic Cashew Cheese, turning it into a savory, piquant creation that holds up well for potlucks and picnics. Whether served with crackers or baguettes or as a filling for sandwiches, this cheese has universal appeal and is a hit with teens.

SUN-DRIED TOMATO AND BASIL cheese

MAKES ABOUT 12 OUNCES

1½ cups Basic Cashew Cheese (page 7), cultured for 1 to 2 days

½ cup finely chopped sun-dried tomatoes (see note)

½ cup slivered fresh basil leaves, firmly packed

3 tablespoons nutritional yeast flakes

2 to 3 cloves garlic, minced

1 teaspoon salt

1. Flavor the cheese.

Put the Basic Cashew Cheese, sun-dried tomatoes, basil, nutritional yeast, 2 cloves of the garlic, and the salt in a large bowl. Mix well. Taste and add more garlic if desired.

2. Form the cheese.

The cheese can be shaped in a mold or be formed into a log or ball by hand. To use a mold, line it with cheesecloth or plastic wrap, pack in the cheese, and smooth the top. Cover or wrap well with plastic wrap and refrigerate for at least 6 hours, until firm.

STORAGE NOTES: Wrapped in plastic wrap and stored in a ziplock bag in the refrigerator, Sun-Dried Tomato and Basil Cheese will keep for about 3 weeks. It can be stored longer, but it will continue to get sharper and stronger in flavor, so taste it occasionally. Once it has achieved the desired flavor, it can be stored in the freezer for up to 4 months.

VARIATION: Substitute Creamy Yogurt Cheese (page 23) for the Basic Cashew Cheese.

NOTE: You can use either dry or oil-packed sun-dried tomatoes. If using the latter, simply drain and chop. If the tomatoes aren't oil-packed, soak them in hot water for about 1 hour, then drain and chop.

Per ounce: calories: 116, protein: 4 g, fat: 8 g, saturated fat: 1 g, carbohydrate: 7 g, sodium: 228 mg, calcium: 14 mg

If you want a vegan cheese that's elegant and creamy, with that distinctive melt-in-your-mouth texture, look no further. This version of Brie is a big hit at parties, whether guests are vegan or not. Be sure to pull it out of the refrigerator an hour or so before serving to bring it to room temperature and allow all cf that divine creaminess to develop. However, do note that because it contains coconut oil, it gets extremely soft in hot conditions and doesn't hold up well for very long. (For a Brie that can withstand warmer temperatures, see the variation on page 39.)

BRIE

See photo facing page 23.

MAKES ABOUT 1½ POUNDS (TWO 6-INCH ROUNDS)

1 pound Basic Cashew Cheese (page 7), cultured for 12 to 24 hours

1 cup refined coconut oil, warmed or melted

1 tablespoon nutritional yeast flakes

¼ teaspoon salt

2 to 3 tablespoons whole peppercorns or chopped fresh herbs (optional)

1. **Flavor the cheese.**
   Put the Basic Cashew Cheese, oil, nutritional yeast, and salt in a blender or food processor and process until smooth and well combined. The mixture will be fairly runny.

2. **Form the cheese.**
   Line two 6-inch cake pans with cheesecloth or plastic wrap. If desired, sprinkle half of the peppercorns or fresh herbs evenly in each pan. Pour the mixture into the pans and spread it evenly. Cover and refrigerate for at least 8 hours, until firm. Let sit at room temperature for 1 hour before serving.

STORAGE NOTES: Wrapped in plastic wrap and stored in a ziplock bag, Brie will keep for about 2 weeks in the refrigerator or 4 months in the freezer.

Per ounce: calories: 149, protein: 2 g, fat: 15 g, saturated fat: 9 g, carbohydrate: 3 g, sodium: 24 mg, calcium: 5 mg

In this recipe, just a few simple ingredients combine to make a vegan version of Gruyère that tastes remarkably like its dairy counterpart. Although it is on the softer side, it makes a fabulous fondue or pasta sauce and beautifully complements pears or sourdough bread. If you're using Soft Gruyère for Cheese Fondue (page 65) or Fettuccine Alfredo with Gruyère and Mushrooms (page 85), there's no need to culture it. Once you've completed step 1, it's ready to go!

soft GRUYÈRE

MAKES ABOUT 1 POUND

2 cups cashews, soaked in water for 3 to 8 hours and drained

½ cup rejuvelac (preferably homemade, page 6)

¼ cup refined coconut oil, warmed or melted

2 tablespoons nutritional yeast flakes

1 to 2 tablespoons medium brown miso

1 teaspoon salt

½ teaspoon xanthan gum

1. Process the ingredients.

Put the cashews, rejuvelac, oil, nutritional yeast, 1 tablespoon of the miso, and the salt and xanthan gum in a blender. Process until smooth and creamy, occasionally stopping to scrape down the blender jar and move the mixture toward the blades. Taste and add more miso if desired.

2. Culture the cheese.

Transfer to a clean glass bowl or container, cover, and let rest at room temperature for 12 to 24 hours, depending on how sharp a flavor you want and the ambient temperature (fermentation will proceed more quickly at warmer temperatures). The cheese will darken slightly, thicken to a spreadable consistency, and develop a rich but not overly tangy flavor. Cover and refrigerate. The cheese will continue to thicken as it chills.

STORAGE NOTES: Stored in a covered container, Soft Gruyère will keep for about 2 months in the refrigerator or 4 months in the freezer.

HARD GRUYÈRE: For a firmer cheese that can be sliced, culture it for 24 to 48 hours, until the desired sharpness and flavor have developed. Transfer to a heavy medium saucepan and stir in 1 tablespoon of carrageenan powder or 2 tablespoons of agar powder with a wooden spoon. Cook over medium heat, stirring almost constantly, until the mixture is glossy and gooey and starts to pull away from the sides of the pan, 4 to 5 minutes. Transfer to a glass or nonreactive metal mold and smooth the top. Let cool completely at room temperature. Cover and refrigerate for at least 6 hours, until firm. *See photos facing pages 22 and 23.*

Per ounce: calories: 142, protein: 4 g, fat: 12 g, saturated fat: 4 g, carbohydrate: 6 g, sodium: 193 mg, calcium: 7 mg

Rich and full flavored, this vegan version of Cheddar continues to age and improve in the refrigerator for weeks or even months. What distinguishes it from store-bought vegan Cheddar equivalents is that the sharpness is not feigned by adding acidic ingredients; it's the result of an actual aging process. I often make this several weeks before I want to serve it because it just keeps getting better—deeper, sharper, and more complex in flavor.

sharp CHEDDAR

See photo facing page 22.

MAKES ABOUT 1 POUND

2 cups raw cashews, soaked in water for 3 to 8 hours and drained

⅔ cup nutritional yeast flakes

½ cup rejuvelac (preferably homemade, page 6)

½ cup canola oil (optional; see note)

1 to 2 tablespoons medium brown miso

1 teaspoon salt

1 tablespoon carrageenan powder, or 2 tablespoons agar powder

½ teaspoon xanthan gum

1. **Process the ingredients.**

Put the cashews, nutritional yeast, rejuvelac, optional oil, 1 tablespoon of the miso, and the salt in a blender. Process until smooth and creamy, occasionally stopping to scrape down the blender jar and move the mixture toward the blades. Taste and add more miso if desired.

2. **Culture the cheese.**

Transfer the mixture to a clean glass bowl or container, cover, and let rest at room temperature for 24 to 72 hours, depending on how sharp a flavor you want and the ambient temperature (fermentation will proceed more quickly at warmer temperatures).

3. **Thicken the cheese.**

Transfer the cheese to a heavy medium saucepan and stir in the carrageenan and xanthan gum with a wooden spoon. Cook over medium heat, stirring almost constantly. The mixture will be very thick, grainy, and difficult to stir at first. Keep cooking and stirring until it is smooth and glossy and starts to pull away from the sides of the pan, 3 to 5 minutes.

4. **Form the cheese.**

Transfer to a glass or metal mold and smooth the top. Let cool completely at room temperature. Cover and refrigerate for at least 6 hours, until firm.

Per ounce: calories: 117, protein: 5 g, fat: 8 g, saturated fat: 1 g, carbohydrate: 6 g, sodium: 213 mg, calcium: 10 mg

The only reason I've never aged it more than four months is because I haven't been able to keep it around longer than that! Although it continues to thicken as it ages, the texture remains more like Cheddar cheese left out on a hot day. (In other words, it's not quite as firm as dairy-based Cheddar.) This is a good cheese to have on hand at all times because of its versatility. It's great for adding to tacos and sandwiches, serving with crackers, and making cheese sauces.

STORAGE NOTES: Stored in a covered container, soft Sharp Cheddar will keep for about 4 months in the refrigerator or freezer. To store hard Sharp Cheddar, wrap it in plastic wrap and put it in a ziplock bag; it will keep for the same amount of time and will become increasingly firm, especially after 3 months.

CROCK-STYLE CHEDDAR: For a softer, spreadable "crock-style" cheese, omit the carrageenan and xanthan gum. After step 2, cover and refrigerate. The cheese will thicken as it chills, but it won't be firm enough for slicing.

NOTE: The optional oil will improve the cheese's ability to melt and give it a smoother mouthfeel. However, I generally don't use the oil, and if you're looking for a cheese that melts well, I recommend that you make the Meltable Cheddar (page 43). Omitting the oil won't affect the flavor of the cheese, and it will still soften if heated. If you wish to heat the cheese, be aware that a skin will form on top, so it is best to spread the warm cheese with a knife.

This looks and tastes like its dairy counterpart: fresh mozzarella made from buffalo's milk, formed into balls, and packed in brine. Serve this cheese in Caprese Salad (page 67) or use it in a caprese sandwich—like the salad, made with freshly sliced tomatoes, fresh basil, and a drizzle of olive oil and balsamic vinegar. When baked, this cheese softens but doesn't really melt, so if you're making pizza or a dish like lasagne, use Meltable Mozzarella (page 44) or Meltable Muenster (page 41) instead.

fresh MOZZARELLA

MAKES ABOUT 1 POUND

2 cups raw cashews, soaked in water for 3 to 8 hours and drained

½ cup rejuvelac (preferably homemade, page 6)

1 teaspoon plus 1 pinch salt

½ to 1 teaspoon xanthan gum

⅔ cup water

1 tablespoon agar powder, or 3 tablespoons agar flakes

4 cups ice water

1. Process the ingredients.

Put the cashews, rejuvelac, and a pinch of salt in a blender. Process until smooth and creamy, occasionally stopping to scrape down the blender jar and move the mixture toward the blades. Add ½ teaspoon of the xanthan gum and process until thickened and gooey.

2. Culture the cheese.

Transfer to a clean glass bowl or container, cover, and let rest at room temperature for 8 to 24 hours, depending on how sharp a flavor you want and the ambient temperature (culturing will proceed more quickly at warmer temperatures). Mozzarella should have a mild flavor, so don't let it ferment so long that it becomes tangy.

3. Thicken the cheese.

Transfer the mixture to a blender. Put the ⅔ cup water and the agar in a small saucepan and bring to a boil over medium-high heat. Decrease the heat to medium-low and simmer, whisking occasionally, until the agar is completely dissolved, 3 to 5 minutes. It should not

Per ¼ cup: calories: 108, protein: 3 g, fat: 8 g, saturated fat: 1 g, carbohydrate: 6 g, sodium: 25 mg, calcium: 11 mg

be cloudy or grainy. Pour into the blender and process until smooth and thoroughly combined. For a stretchier consistency in the final product, add an additional ¼ to ½ teaspoon of xanthan gum and process until thoroughly combined.

4. Form the cheese.

To make a brine, put the ice water and 1 teaspoon of salt in a large bowl and stir until the salt dissolves. Form the cheese into balls using a small ice-cream scoop, dropping them into the brine as you go. They will harden almost instantly. Cover and refrigerate, keeping the cheese stored in the brine.

STORAGE NOTES: Covered and stored in the brine, Fresh Mozzarella will keep for about 2 weeks in the refrigerator. The brine will help it retain its shape and preserve its freshness.

The addition of beer and chives to Cheddar cheese creates a robust, complex flavor, accentuating the nutty notes of the cheese. This cheese goes well with hearty foods and, of course, a good beer. To make a rarebit sauce that's great over potatoes and broccoli, heat this cheese with just enough beer to achieve a pourable consistency.

PUB CHEDDAR with chives

MAKES ABOUT 1¼ POUNDS

2 cups raw cashews, soaked in water for 3 to 8 hours and drained

⅔ cup nutritional yeast flakes

½ cup rejuvelac (preferably homemade, page 6)

1 to 2 tablespoons medium brown miso

1 teaspoon salt

¾ cup ale or dark beer

1 tablespoon carrageenan powder, or 2 tablespoons agar powder

½ cup minced fresh chives

1. **Process the ingredients.**

Put the cashews, nutritional yeast, rejuvelac, 1 tablespoon of the miso, and the salt in a blender. Process until smooth and creamy, occasionally stopping to scrape down the blender jar and move the mixture toward the blades. Taste and add more miso if desired.

2. **Culture the cheese.**

Transfer to a clean glass bowl or container, cover, and let rest at room temperature for 24 to 48 hours, depending on how sharp a flavor you want and the ambient temperature (fermentation will proceed more quickly at warmer temperatures). At this point, the cheese can be refrigerated for up to 48 hours.

3. **Thicken the cheese.**

Pour the ale into a heavy medium saucepan and stir in the carrageenan with a wooden spoon. Bring to a simmer over medium-high heat. Stir in the cheese. Decrease the heat to medium-low and cook, stirring constantly, until smooth and glossy, 3 to 5 minutes. Remove from the heat and stir in the chives.

4. **Form the cheese.**

Pour into a glass or nonreactive metal mold and smooth the top. Let cool completely at room temperature. Cover and refrigerate for at least 24 hours.

STORAGE NOTES: Wrapped in plastic wrap and stored in a ziplock bag, Pub Cheddar with Chives will keep for about 4 months in the refrigerator or freezer.

Per ounce: calories: 98, protein: 4 g, fat: 7 g, saturated fat: 1 g, carbohydrate: 5 g, sodium: 155 mg, calcium: 8 mg

This is similar to Almond Ricotta (page 47) but is a little richer and more complex in flavor because it's cultured. Macadamia Ricotta makes a spectacular filling for Stuffed Squash Blossoms (page 72) and is also fantastic in lasagne or ravioli.

MACADAMIA ricotta

MAKES ABOUT 3½ CUPS

2 cups raw macadamia nuts, soaked in water for 8 to 12 hours and drained

1 cup water

Large pinch salt

1. Process the ingredients.

Put the macadamia nuts, water, and salt in a blender. Process until smooth and creamy, occasionally stopping to scrape down the blender jar and move the mixture toward the blades. The mixture will be quite soft.

2. Culture the cheese.

Transfer to a clean glass bowl or container, cover, and let rest at room temperature for 12 to 24 hours, depending on the ambient temperature, until flavorful but not too tangy. (Culturing will proceed more quickly at warmer temperatures.) Cover and refrigerate.

STORAGE NOTES: Stored in a covered container, Macadamia Ricotta will keep for about 1 week in the refrigerator or 4 months in the freezer.

Per ¼ cup: calories: 137, protein: 2 g, fat: 15 g, saturated fat: 2 g, carbohydrate: 1 g, sodium: 31 mg, calcium: 16 mg

If you've craved cheesecakes, rich cream cheese frosting, and other sweets traditionally made with cream cheese (which you'll find recipes for in chapter 9), this recipe will come to your rescue. The basic version below isn't sweet, however, so you can also enjoy it on bagels or in savory dishes. In fact, you can use it in just about any recipe that calls for cream cheese. Only a bit of nondairy yogurt is needed to culture this versatile cheese.

cashew CREAM CHEESE

MAKES ABOUT 1 POUND (ABOUT 2 CUPS)

2 cups raw cashews, soaked in water for 8 hours and drained

½ cup water

2 tablespoons plain, unsweetened nondairy yogurt (preferably homemade, page 56)

Pinch salt

1. **Process the ingredients.**

   Put the cashews, water, nondairy yogurt, and salt in a blender. Process until smooth and creamy, occasionally stopping to scrape down the blender jar and move the mixture toward the blades.

2. **Culture the cheese.**

   Transfer to a clean glass bowl or container, cover, and let rest at room temperature for 24 to 48 hours, depending on how sharp a flavor you want and the ambient temperature (culturing will proceed more quickly at warmer temperatures). For use in cheesecakes that will be sweetened, allowing it to culture for a full 48 hours will create a tanginess that will nicely complement the sweetener. Cover and refrigerate. The cheese will get firmer as it chills.

STORAGE NOTES: Stored in a covered container, Cashew Cream Cheese will keep for about 2 weeks in the refrigerator or 4 months in the freezer.

Per ounce (2 tablespoons): calories: 106, protein: 4 g, fat: 8 g, saturated fat: 1 g, carbohydrate: 5 g, sodium: 11 mg, calcium: 9 mg

MASCARPONE: The Italian version of cream cheese and the star ingredient in tiramisu, mascarpone is similar to cream cheese, but a little sweeter, milder, and typically softer. To make a nondairy version of mascarpone, allow the cashew mixture to culture for only 12 to 24 hours—long enough to thicken and develop some flavor, but not so long that it gets tangy. It should have a sweet, mild flavor.

FIRM CASHEW CREAM CHEESE: To make a firm, block-type cream cheese, press the cheese after it's cultured. Line a small sieve or colander with a double layer of cheesecloth, using enough cheesecloth that it hangs over the edges. Put the sieve over a bowl. Put the cheese in the sieve and wrap the ends of the cheesecloth over the top. Put a plate on top and put a 5- to 10-pound weight on the plate—a clean river rock, a container of water, a cast-iron skillet, or whatever you have handy. Let stand at room temperature for about 24 hours to press much of the liquid out of the cheese. (Discard the liquid.) The resulting cheese will be quite firm. Use as is, or flavor with chives, herbs, or garlic.

Draining yogurt is an easy way to make a thick but spreadable cheese that can replicate sour cream, crème fraîche, cream cheese, or chèvre, depending on how it is flavored. The longer it drains, the thicker it will get. The actual hands-on time is minimal, but you do need to allow twelve to twenty-four hours for draining. It's best to flavor this cheese, as it is fairly bland on its own. I offer two methods here: one using a cheese bag and the other using a sieve or colander lined with cheesecloth. The first will allow more liquid to drain off, resulting in a thicker cheese but a lower yield. Even when using the same method, the amount of liquid that drains from the yogurt differs from batch to batch, so it's difficult to give an exact yield for this recipe.

basic YOGURT CHEESE

MAKES ABOUT 1½ CUPS

4 cups plain, unsweetened nondairy yogurt (preferably homemade, page 56)

TO USE A CHEESE BAG: If you have a cheese bag, simply pour the yogurt into the bag and hang it over a bowl (or tie it over the kitchen faucet so the liquid drains into the sink). Let it drain at room temperature for 24 hours or more until liquid is no longer draining from the bag and the yogurt cheese is very thick. There should be no more than 1½ cups of solids.

TO USE A SIEVE OR COLANDER AND CHEESECLOTH: Line a sieve or colander with a double layer of cheesecloth, using enough cheesecloth that it hangs over the edges. Put the sieve over a bowl and pour in the yogurt. Cover loosely with the cheesecloth and let the yogurt drain at room temperature for at least 12 hours, until the yogurt cheese is somewhat thick but still soft. There should be no more than 2 cups of solids. Use as is for sour cream or crème fraîche. To thicken it further, gather the corners of the cheesecloth and tie them a knot at the top to form a bag. Hang the bag over a bowl or from the faucet and let drain for 12 to 24 hours, until the cheese reaches the desired consistency.

STORAGE NOTES: Stored in a covered container, Basic Yogurt Cheese will keep for about 2 weeks in the refrigerator or about 4 months in the freezer.

Per ½ cup: calories: 200, protein: 8 g, fat: 5 g, saturated fat: 0 g, carbohydrate: 29 g, sodium: 40 mg, calcium: 160 mg

sandwich made with Hard Gruyère, *page 13,* and Sharp Cheddar, *page 14*

Clockwise from top left: **Air-Dried Gouda,** *page 28,* **Hard Gruyère,** *page 13,*
Brie with whole peppercorns, *page 12,* **Boursin,** *page 10,*
Sun-Dried Tomato and Garlic Cream Cheese *page 24,* **and Meltable Muenster,** *page 41*

A few simple seasonings turn drained nondairy yogurt into a thick, creamy, spreadable cheese that's great on bagels and sandwiches or in ravioli, lasagne, and other savory dishes. Because the yield of the Basic Yogurt Cheese recipe is variable depending on the yogurt used and the draining time and method, it's difficult to give exact quantities for the seasonings. Start with the amounts listed and increase them as needed to achieve the desired flavor.

creamy YOGURT CHEESE

MAKES 1 TO 1½ CUPS

1 to 1½ cups Basic Yogurt Cheese (page 22)

2 to 3 tablespoons nutritional yeast flakes

1 tablespoon freshly squeezed lemon juice, plus more as desired

1 teaspoon salt, plus more as desired

1. Flavor the cheese.

Put the Basic Yogurt Cheese, 2 tablespoons of the nutritional yeast, and the lemon juice and salt in a medium bowl. Mix well. Season with the remaining tablespoon of nutritional yeast if desired and additional lemon juice and salt to taste.

2. Form the cheese.

Line a small glass or nonreactive metal mold with cheesecloth or plastic wrap. Pack in the cheese and smooth the top. Cover and refrigerate for at least 8 hours, until firm. When ready to serve, use the cheesecloth to help unmold the cheese.

STORAGE NOTES: Stored in a covered container, Creamy Yogurt Cheese will keep for about 2 weeks in the refrigerator or 4 months in the freezer.

TRUFFLED YOGURT CHEESE: Add ½ to 1 teaspoon truffle oil when flavoring the cheese; white truffle oil has a slightly stronger flavor than black. If you want to splurge, also stir in a bit of freshly shaved truffle.

Per ½ cup: calories: 242, protein: 13 g, fat: 6 g, saturated fat: 0 g, carbohydrate: 35 g, sodium: 896 mg, calcium: 161 mg

This is a great way to use up Fresh Mozzarella or Cashew Cream Cheese that becomes too sharp after an extended time in the refrigerator. The pungent garlic and tangy sun-dried tomatoes play upon the sharpness and create a rich, flavorful, reddish cheese that's great on crackers or sandwiches.

sun-dried tomato and garlic CREAM CHEESE See photo facing page 23.

MAKES 10 TO 12 OUNCES

8 ounces Fresh Mozzarella (page 16) **or Cashew Cream Cheese** (page 20)

½ cup sun-dried tomatoes (see note)

3 cloves garlic

1 teaspoon salt

Put the Fresh Mozzerella, sun-dried tomatoes, garlic, and salt in a food processor. Process until fairly creamy, leaving the sun-dried tomatoes slightly chunky or processing longer for a smoother consistency. Transfer to a container, cover, and refrigerate.

STORAGE NOTES: Stored in a covered container, Sun-Dried Tomato and Garlic Cream Cheese will keep for about 3 weeks in the refrigerator or 4 months in the freezer.

NOTE: You can use either dry or oil-packed sun-dried tomatoes. If using the latter, simply drain them before putting them in the food processor. If the tomatoes aren't oil-packed, soak them in hot water for about 1 hour, then drain them well before putting them in the food processor.

Per ounce (2 tablespoons): calories: 86, protein: 3 g, fat: 6 g, saturated fat: 1 g, carbohydrate: 5 g, sodium: 263 mg, calcium: 12 mg

This was the very first vegan cheese I ever made, over thirty years ago. After a week of marinating, the tofu develops a spreadable, buttery, cheeselike consistency. It's wonderful alongside grilled veggies and on croûtes, or served in croustade. It can also be blended to make aïoli, salad dressings, and sauces.

TOFU cheese

MAKES ABOUT 1 POUND

1 cup medium brown miso

½ cup dry white wine

¼ cup mirin

1 pound firm regular tofu, sliced
½ inch thick

1. **Make the marinade.**
Put the miso, wine, and mirin in a shallow pan and mix with a whisk or fork until thoroughly blended.

2. **Marinate the tofu.**
Submerge the tofu slices in the marinade, making sure all of them are well coated on all sides. Cover and refrigerate for 1 week. Remove the tofu from the marinade gently, as it will be very delicate. Fill a bowl with water and rinse the tofu pieces carefully in the water to remove any residual marinade. Discard the marinade.

STORAGE NOTES: Stored in a covered container, Tofu Cheese will keep for about 3 weeks in the refrigerator.

SHARP TOFU CHÈVRE: After rinsing, put the tofu slices in a lidded glass storage container. Pour in just enough freshly squeezed lemon juice to cover the tofu. Cover and refrigerate for at least 24 hours, until pungent and sharp tasting.

TOFU FETA: After rinsing, put the tofu slices in a lidded glass storage container. Pour in just enough extra-virgin olive oil to cover the tofu and sprinkle with 1 teaspoon of salt. Gently turn the slices over to evenly distribute the salt. Cover and refrigerate for at least 24 hours.

Per 2 ounces (¼ cup): calories: 83, protein: 8 g, fat: 4 g, saturated fat: 1 g, carbohydrate: 3 g, sodium: 324 mg, calcium: 100 mg

2

Air-Dried Cheeses

In the dairy world, most hard cheeses are air-dried and aged for a period of days, weeks, or months. After the curds are separated from the whey, they are pressed to expel most of the liquid. The firming process continues over time as the cheese is dried out by being exposed to air. The size of the cheese and the duration of air-drying determine how hard the final cheese is, yielding a variety of textures from creamy but sliceable Emmentaler or Gouda to extremely hard and easy-to-grate Parmesan. To a certain extent, a similar process is possible with vegan cheeses.

When air-drying vegan cheeses, there are several key points to keep in mind. It is critical to salt the surface of the cheese to suppress unwanted growth of mold or bacteria. Salt also contributes to the development of flavor, so all of the cheeses in this chapter are sprinkled or rubbed with salt prior to air-drying. The salting process is generally repeated after a few days, and it's especially important to do so if the humidity is high. The ambient temperature is also critical. These cheeses require cool temperatures for aging, especially if aged for more than three or four days. Something akin to a wine cave is ideal (typically around 55 degrees F), although I've had perfectly good results when aging cheeses in a cool room at around 65 degrees F. A cool basement or pantry can also work well.

Another point to keep in mind is that the entire surface of the cheese should be exposed to air, not just the top and sides. The best way to do this is to put cheeses on a rack, such as a wire rack for cooling baked goods. A wire rack with a grid pattern works especially well.

The longest I've air-dried a cheese is four months. I finally gave in and ate it, but during the entire aging time I never had any issues with mold of any kind. That cheese was based on Basic Cashew Cheese (page 7), and while it was good, I wasn't thrilled with the texture. It was somewhat too crumbly and grainy due to the fact that Basic Cashew Cheese is made of ground-up cashews with only minimal liquid. While this is fine for a cheese aged for only a few days, over a period of weeks the solids in the cheese simply turn grainy.

After some trial and error, I realized that air-dried cheeses need a higher liquid content if they are to have a creamier texture. This led to an entirely new path of experimentation, resulting in the cheese recipes in this chapter. Many of these cheeses contain nondairy yogurt, a bit of oil or wine, or a combination of these more liquid ingredients. I look forward to many more years of experimentation on this path.

This Gouda develops a nice rind that surrounds a creamy and smooth but firm interior. It's actually tasty if eaten right away, although it's very soft at that stage and doesn't really resemble Gouda. After several days of air-drying, however, the flavor comes alive and the cheese becomes firm enough to slice.

air-dried GOUDA

See photo facing page 23.

MAKES ABOUT 1¼ POUNDS

2 cups raw cashews, soaked in water for 3 to 8 hours and drained

1 cup plain, unsweetened nondairy yogurt (preferably homemade, page 56)

½ cup rejuvelac (preferably homemade, page 6)

⅓ cup canola oil or refined coconut oil (optional; see note)

¼ cup dry white wine

3 tablespoons tapioca flour

2 tablespoons nutritional yeast flakes

1 tablespoon medium brown miso

1 tablespoon carrageenan powder, or 2 tablespoons agar powder

2½ teaspoons salt

1. **Process the ingredients.**

Put the cashews, yogurt, rejuvelac, optional oil, wine, tapioca flour, nutritional yeast, miso, carrageenan, and 1½ teaspoons of the salt in a blender. Process until smooth and creamy, occasionally stopping to scrape down the blender jar and move the mixture toward the blades.

2. **Cook the mixture.**

Pour the mixture into a heavy medium saucepan. Cook over medium heat, stirring almost constantly with a wooden spoon. The mixture will become lumpy, then, after 3 to 5 minutes, it should be smooth, stretchy, and bubbly. If you added the optional oil, it will also develop a slight sheen.

3. **Form the cheese.**

Pour the mixture into a glass or nonreactive metal mold and smooth the top. Let cool completely at room temperature. Cover and refrigerate for at least 4 hours, until firm.

4. **Salt the cheese.**

Run a knife around the edge of the mold, then gently pry the cheese out and put it on a plate. Wash your hands well, rinse them thoroughly, and while they are still wet, sprinkle the remaining teaspoon of salt over your palms. Rub the salt over the entire surface of the cheese.

Per ounce: calories: 103, protein: 4 g, fat: 7 g, saturated fat: 1 g, carbohydrate: 7 g, sodium: 318 mg, calcium: 12 mg

5. Air-dry the cheese.

Put the cheese on a drying rack in a cool place with good air circulation. Let air-dry for 5 days. It will develop a rind and become firmer. Taste it to see if it is flavorful and firm enough. If not, let it air-dry for 2 to 3 more days, until it has the desired texture and flavor.

STORAGE NOTES: Wrapped in plastic wrap and stored in a ziplock bag, Air-Dried Gouda will keep for about 1 month in the refrigerator or 4 months in the freezer.

NOTE: Although the oil is optional, including it in the recipe will improve the mouthfeel of the cheese.

This Cheddar undergoes double culturing—first for two to three days prior to forming the cheese, then for several more days as it air-dries. The reward is a sliceable, sharp Cheddar that's perfect for sandwiches or for a cheese plate.

air-dried CHEDDAR

MAKES ABOUT 1 POUND 6 OUNCES

2 cups cashews, soaked in water for 3 to 8 hours and drained

1 cup plain, unsweetened nondairy yogurt (preferably homemade, see page 56)

¾ cup rejuvelac (preferably homemade, page 6)

⅔ cup nutritional yeast flakes

⅓ cup medium brown miso

3 tablespoons canola oil (optional; see note)

1½ teaspoons salt, plus more as needed

5 tablespoons tapioca flour

1½ tablespoons carrageenan powder, or 3 tablespoons agar powder

1. Process the ingredients.

Put the cashews, yogurt, rejuvelac, nutritional yeast, miso, optional oil, and 1 teaspoon of the salt in a blender. Process until smooth and creamy, occasionally stopping to scrape down the blender jar and move the mixture toward the blades.

2. Culture the cheese.

Transfer to a clean glass bowl or container, cover, and let rest at room temperature for 36 to 48 hours, until the mixture has a deep, sharp flavor.

3. Thicken the cheese.

Transfer the mixture to a heavy medium saucepan and whisk in the tapioca flour and carrageenan. Bring to a simmer over medium-low heat, stirring constantly with a wooden spoon. As the mixture heats, it will become stretchy. Continue to cook, stirring constantly, until smooth and slightly glossy, 2 to 5 minutes.

4. Form the cheese.

Pour into a glass or nonreactive metal mold and smooth the top. Let cool completely at room temperature. Cover and refrigerate for at least 4 hours, until firm.

Per ounce: calories: 118, protein: 6 g, fat: 7 g, saturated fat: 1 g, carbohydrate: 9 g, sodium: 288 mg, calcium: 13 mg

5. Salt the cheese.

Run a knife around the edge of the mold, then gently pry the cheese out and put it on a plate. Wash your hands well, rinse them thoroughly, and while they are still wet, sprinkle the remaining $\frac{1}{2}$ teaspoon of salt over your palms. Rub the salt over the entire surface of the cheese.

6. Air-dry the cheese.

Put the cheese on a drying rack in a cool place with good air circulation. Let air-dry for 4 days. The surface may crack a little. As it dries, the cheese will become firmer and easier to slice. Taste it to see if it's sufficiently sharp and dry. If not, turn the cheese over, sprinkle $\frac{1}{8}$ to $\frac{1}{4}$ teaspoon of salt evenly over the entire surface, and let it air-dry for 1 to 3 more days.

STORAGE NOTES: Wrapped in plastic wrap and stored in a ziplock bag, Air-Dried Cheddar will keep for about 1 month in the refrigerator or 4 months in the freezer.

NOTE: Although the oil is optional, including it in the recipe will improve the mouthfeel of the cheese.

This cheese has a flavor quite reminiscent of Swiss cheese. However, there are no holes—sorry!

air-dried EMMENTALER

MAKES ABOUT 1 POUND

1 cup plain, unsweetened nondairy yogurt (preferably homemade, page 56)

½ cup raw cashews

6 tablespoons tapioca flour

⅓ cup sauerkraut, drained

¼ cup canola oil

¼ cup dry white wine

¼ cup rejuvelac (preferably homemade, page 6)

1½ teaspoons salt

¾ cup water

4 teaspoons agar powder, or ¼ cup agar flakes

1. Process the ingredients.

Put the yogurt, cashews, tapioca flour, sauerkraut, oil, wine, rejuvelac, and 1 teaspoon of the salt in a blender. Process until smooth and creamy, occasionally stopping to scrape down the blender jar and move the mixture toward the blades.

2. Culture the cheese.

Transfer to a clean glass bowl or container, cover, and let rest at room temperature for 24 to 48 hours, until slightly sharp in flavor.

3. Thicken the cheese.

Put the water and agar in a heavy medium saucepan and whisk until well mixed. Bring to a boil over medium heat. Pour in the yogurt mixture and mix well with a wooden spoon. Decrease the heat to medium and cook, stirring frequently, until thick, gooey, and glossy, 2 to 5 minutes.

4. Form the cheese.

Pour into a glass or nonreactive metal mold and smooth the top. Let cool completely at room temperature. Cover and refrigerate for at least 4 hours, until firm.

Per ounce: calories: 83, protein: 1 g, fat: 6 g, saturated fat: 1 g, carbohydrate: 6 g, sodium: 237 mg, calcium: 16 mg

5. Salt the cheese.

Run a knife around the edge of the mold, then gently pry the cheese out and put it on a plate. Sprinkle the remaining ½ teaspoon of salt evenly over the entire surface of the cheese.

6. Air-dry the cheese.

Put the cheese on a drying rack in a cool place with good air circulation. Let air-dry for 2 to 3 days. The cheese will get firmer as it dries.

STORAGE NOTES: Wrapped in plastic wrap and stored in a ziplock bag, Air-Dried Emmentaler will keep for about 2 months in the refrigerator or 4 months in the freezer

Patience and the right environment are required, but it is possible to make vegan Parmesan cheese that's sharp, nutty, and hard enough to grate. It has a darker color than its dairy counterpart but is entirely satisfying over pasta, vegetables, or a Caesar salad. As a bonus, it will keep for several months in the refrigerator.

air-dried PARMESAN

MAKES ABOUT 8 OUNCES

2 cups Basic Yogurt Cheese (page 22)

6 tablespoons nutritional yeast flakes

¼ cup medium brown miso

½ teaspoon salt, plus more as needed

1. **Flavor the cheese.**
Put the Basic Yogurt Cheese, nutritional yeast, and miso in a medium bowl. Mix well.

2. **Form the cheese.**
Put a piece of parchment paper over a drying rack. Gather the mixture into a ball and transfer it to the covered rack. Flatten it to form a brick or round about ½ inch thick.

3. **Salt the cheese.**
Sprinkle about ¼ teaspoon of the salt evenly over the top.

4. **Air-dry the cheese.**
Put the rack and cheese in a cool place with good air circulation. Let air-dry for 24 hours. The cheese will become somewhat firm, and the top will be dry enough that the cheese can be flipped over. Use the parchment paper to flip the cheese over directly onto the rack; discard the parchment paper. Wash your hands well, rinse them thoroughly, and while they are still wet, sprinkle the remaining ¼ teaspoon of salt over your palms. Rub the salt over the top and sides of the cheese. Let air-dry for 10 to 14 days, flipping the cheese over every 2 days and checking daily for mold or other unwanted surface growth. If there's any sign of mold or other growth, scrape or cut it off as soon as it appears and sprinkle a bit more salt on the surface. The cheese is ready when it is hard and quite dry throughout (slice and check).

Per ounce: calories: 148, protein: 10 g, fat: 4 g, saturated fat: 0 g, carbohydrate: 19 g, sodium: 456 mg, calcium: 80 mg

STORAGE NOTES: Wrapped in plastic wrap and stored in a ziplock bag, Air-Dried Parmesan will keep for about 4 months in the refrigerator or freezer.

AIR-DRIED PARMESAN WITH PINE NUTS: Adding pine nuts will contribute a nutty flavor to this cheese. Put the Basic Yogurt Cheese, nutritional yeast, miso, and ⅓ cup of pine nuts in a blender. Process until smooth and creamy. Form, salt, and air-dry the cheese as directed in the main recipe.

I can't put my finger on what this cheese resembles in terms of its dairy counterpart, but I'm sure I've had something like this in the past. This air-dried cheese has a brown rind, a creamy interior, and a strong, nutty, piquant flavor. It goes well with beer and other beverages that hold their own against a slightly salty, full-flavored cheese.

air-dried **PIQUANT BROWN CHEESE**

MAKES ABOUT 13 OUNCES

2 cups raw cashews, soaked in water for 3 to 8 hours and drained

½ cup rejuvelac (preferably homemade, page 6)

2 cubes fermented tofu (see note)

1 tablespoon umeboshi paste

1 teaspoon salt

1. **Process the ingredients.**

   Put the cashews, rejuvelac, fermented tofu, umeboshi paste, and ½ teaspoon of the salt in a blender. Process until smooth and creamy, occasionally stopping to scrape down the blender jar and move the mixture toward the blades.

2. **Culture the cheese.**

   Transfer to a clean glass bowl or container, cover, and let rest at room temperature for 24 hours.

3. **Form the cheese.**

   Put a piece of parchment paper over a drying rack. Gather the mixture into a ball and transfer it to the covered rack. Form it into a dome shape about 2 inches high in the middle.

4. **Salt the cheese.**

   Sprinkle about ¼ teaspoon of the salt evenly over the top.

5. **Air-dry the cheese.**

   Put the rack and cheese in a cool place with good air circulation. Let air-dry for 24 to 36 hours, until a crust has formed. Use the parchment paper to flip the cheese over directly onto the rack; discard the parchment paper. Sprinkle the remaining ¼ teaspoon of salt evenly over the cheese. Let air-dry for 24 hours. Turn the cheese over so that the domed side is on top again. Let air-dry for 10 to 12 days, until a crust has formed and the cheese is brown throughout (slice and check).

Per ounce: calories: 133, protein: 4 g, fat: 10 g, saturated fat: 2 g, carbohydrate: 6 g, sodium: 294 mg, calcium: 10 mg

STORAGE NOTES: Wrapped in plastic wrap and stored in a ziplock bag, Air-Dried Piquant Brown Cheese will keep for about 2 months in the refrigerator or 4 months in the freezer.

NOTE: Fermented tofu, a very strong-tasting product available in Asian grocery stores, is cubed tofu preserved in a mixture of wine, vinegar, salt, and other ingredients. It's available in different flavors; for this recipe, use a plain version.

The king and queen of cheeses, Camembert and Brie are comparable in flavor and appearance. Tradition-ally, they are made using similar ingredients and techniques, but they hail from different parts of France. Some people say that Camembert has a slightly stronger flavor, so in this recipe the base mixture is cultured a bit longer than the base of the Air-Dried Brie variation (page 39).

air-dried CAMEMBERT

MAKES ABOUT 1 POUND
(ONE 6-INCH ROUND)

1 cup plain, unsweetened nondairy yogurt (preferably homemade, page 56)

1 cup raw cashews, soaked in water for 3 to 8 hours and drained

½ cup rejuvelac (preferably homemade, page 6)

¼ cup canola oil

2 tablespoons nutritional yeast flakes

1½ teaspoons salt

3 tablespoons tapioca flour

1 teaspoon carrageenan powder, or 2 teaspoons agar powder

1. **Process the ingredients.**
Put the yogurt, cashews, rejuvelac, oil, nutritional yeast, and 1 tea-spoon of the salt in a blender. Process until smooth and creamy.

2. **Culture the cheese.**
Transfer to a clean glass bowl or container, cover, and let rest at room temperature for 24 to 36 hours, until the mixture has achieved the desired sharpness.

3. **Thicken the cheese.**
Transfer the mixture to a heavy medium saucepan and whisk in the tapioca flour and carrageenan. Cook over medium heat, stirring constantly with a wooden spoon, until bubbling, very thick, and shiny, 3 to 5 minutes.

4. **Form the cheese.**
Line a 6-inch round cake pan with cheesecloth or plastic wrap. Pour the mixture into the pan and spread it evenly. Let cool completely at room temperature. Cover and refrigerate for at least 4 hours, until firm enough to remove.

Per ounce: calories: 104, protein: 3 g, fat: 8 g, saturated fat: 1 g, carbohydrate: 6 g, sodium: 205 mg, calcium: 14 mg

Whatever you choose to call this cheese, once it has aged you'll have a lovely round with a thin rind and a creamy, gooey interior. Although it is delicious as is at room temperature, it's even more spectacular served warm, prepared as Brie en Croûte with Dried Fruit and Nuts (page 80). Unlike the Brie in chapter 1 (page 12), this variation holds up well in warm weather.

5. Salt the cheese.

Use the cheesecloth to gently remove the cheese from the pan. Put it on a drying rack and discard the cheesecloth. Wash your hands well, rinse them thoroughly, and while they are still wet sprinkle the remaining ½ teaspoon of salt over your palms. Gently rub the salt over the entire surface of the cheese.

6. Air-dry the cheese.

Put the rack and cheese in a cool place with good air circulation. Let air-dry for 24 to 48 hours, until a slight skin has formed but the inside is still soft and gooey (gently press the top to check).

STORAGE NOTES: Wrapped in plastic wrap and stored in a ziplock bag, Camembert will keep for about 2 weeks in the refrigerator or 4 months in the freezer.

HEMPSEED CAMEMBERT: Substitute ½ cup hempseeds for the entire 1 cup of cashews. Hempseeds are higher in fat, so this will create a very rich, gooey cheese. Note that it may have a slight green tint.

AIR-DRIED BRIE: Follow the instructions in the main recipe, but in step 2, culture for only 12 hours so the flavor doesn't become too tangy.

3

Meltable cheeses

While many of the recipes in chapters 1 and 2 make fabulous cheeses suitable for a cheese platter or just plain noshing, this is the go-to chapter for cheeses that melt and, to a degree, stretch. As with their dairy counterparts, it is the fat content (oil in this case) that helps with melting, so these are higher in fat than most of the cheeses in this book. However, if you've been craving a gooey, melty, stretchy topping for your pizza or gratin and are willing to occasionally toss caution to the wind, you're in the right place. Some of these cheeses are also delicious eaten plain—no melting required!

A key way in which these recipes vary from those in chapters 1, 2, and 4 is in the choice of solidifying agents. While many of the other recipes offer the alternative of using either carrageenan or agar, these don't. Carrageenan softens more readily than agar when reheated and therefore is the thickener of choice for cheeses that will melt. As with the other cheeses in this book, the meltable cheeses continue to get sharper the longer they are cultured and even while stored in the refrigerator.

This cheese has a creamy, smooth, buttery texture that melts in your mouth—or on a hot sandwich. Served cold, it pairs beautifully with apples and pears. Because Muenster is a mild cheese, the base for this vegan version isn't cultured, making for a meltable cheese that's almost instant!

meltable MUENSTER

See photo facing page 23.

MAKES ABOUT 1 POUND

1 cup plain, unsweetened nondairy yogurt (preferably homemade, page 56)

½ cup water

⅓ cup canola oil

¼ cup tapioca flour

1 tablespoon nutritional yeast flakes

1 tablespoon carrageenan powder

1 teaspoon salt

1. Process the ingredients.

Put all the ingredients in a blender. Process until smooth and creamy, occasionally stopping to scrape down the blender jar and move the mixture toward the blades.

2. Cook the mixture.

Pour the mixture into a heavy medium saucepan. Cook over medium heat, stirring almost constantly with a wire whisk, until very smooth, thick, gooey, and glossy, 3 to 5 minutes. It's important to cook it until there is an obvious sheen, or the cheese won't melt well.

3. Form the cheese.

Pour the mixture into a glass or nonreactive metal mold and smooth the top. Let cool completely at room temperature. Cover and refrigerate for at least 3 hours, until firm.

STORAGE NOTES: Wrapped in plastic wrap and stored in a ziplock bag, Meltable Muenster will keep for about 4 weeks in the refrigerator.

NOTE: If you want a reddish tint on the surface of the cheese to resemble traditional Muenster, lightly sprinkle paprika on the outside.

Per ounce: calories: 57, protein: 1 g, fat: 5 g, saturated fat: 0 g, carbohydrate: 3 g, sodium: 136 mg, calcium: 9 mg

This vegan cheese has the slightly crumbly appearance of dairy-based dry Monterey Jack and really does melt like conventional cheese. It's ideal for grilled cheese sandwiches, or you can defy convention and use it to top a pizza. When baked, it bubbles and browns beautifully.

meltable MONTEREY JACK

MAKES ABOUT 1 POUND

1 cup plain, unsweetened nondairy yogurt (preferably homemade, page 56)

½ cup water

½ cup canola oil

1½ teaspoons salt

3 tablespoons tapioca flour

2 tablespoons carrageenan powder

1. **Process the ingredients.**
Put the yogurt, water, oil, and salt in a blender. Process until smooth and creamy, occasionally stopping to scrape down the blender jar and move the mixture toward the blades.

2. **Culture the cheese.**
Transfer to a clean glass bowl or container, cover, and let rest at room temperature for 8 to 24 hours, until mildly sharp in flavor.

3. **Thicken the cheese.**
Transfer to a heavy medium saucepan and whisk in the tapioca flour and carrageenan. Cook over medium heat, stirring almost constantly with the whisk, until the mixture is smooth and glossy and starts to pull away from the sides of the pan, 5 to 10 minutes.

4. **Form the cheese.**
Pour the mixture into a rectangular glass or nonreactive metal mold, such as a loaf pan, and smooth the top. Let cool completely at room temperature. Cover and refrigerate for at least 2 hours, until firm.

STORAGE NOTES: Wrapped in plastic wrap and stored in a ziplock bag, Meltable Monterey Jack will keep for about 6 weeks in the refrigerator.

Per ounce: calories: 77, protein: 0 g, fat: 7 g, saturated fat: 1 g, carbohydrate: 3 g, sodium: 203 mg, calcium: 10 mg

The Sharp Cheddar (page 14), with its complex flavor, is spectacular for a cheese platter, but this is my go-to cheese for grilled cheese sandwiches, vegan omelets, and other gooey delicacies. It doesn't age as well as the Sharp Cheddar, so use it within a few weeks, then make a fresh batch.

meltable CHEDDAR

MAKES ABOUT 1 POUND

1 cup plain, unsweetened nondairy yogurt (preferably homemade, page 56)

½ cup water

6 tablespoons nutritional yeast flakes

⅓ cup canola oil

2 to 3 tablespoons medium brown miso

1 teaspoon salt

5 tablespoons tapioca flour

1½ tablespoons carrageenan powder

½ teaspoon xanthan gum (optional)

1. Process the ingredients.
Put the yogurt, water, nutritional yeast, oil, 2 tablespoons of the miso, and the salt in a blender. Process until smooth and creamy, occasionally stopping to scrape down the blender jar and move the mixture toward the blades. Taste and add more miso if desired.

2. Culture the cheese.
Transfer the mixture to a clean container, cover, and let rest at room temperature for 24 to 48 hours, depending on how sharp a flavor you want.

3. Thicken the cheese.
Transfer to a heavy medium saucepan and whisk in the tapioca flour and carrageenan. For a stretchier consistency, whisk in the optional xanthan gum. Cook over medium heat, stirring almost constantly with the whisk, until very smooth, thick, gooey, and glossy, 3 to 5 minutes. It's important to cook it until there is an obvious sheen, or the cheese won't melt well.

4. Form the cheese.
Pour the mixture into a glass or nonreactive metal mold and smooth the top. Cover and let cool completely at room temperature. Refrigerate for at least 3 hours, until firm.

STORAGE NOTES: Wrapped in plastic wrap and stored in a ziplock bag, Meltable Cheddar will keep for about 4 weeks in the refrigerator.

Per ounce: calories: 77, protein: 3 g, fat: 5 g, saturated fat: 0 g, carbohydrate: 6 g, sodium: 231 mg, calcium: 9 mg

Choices, choices. I offer two recipes for mozzarella in this book, one made from cashews, and this one, which is made from nondairy yogurt. Which to choose? For Caprese Salad (page 67), my choice would be Fresh Mozzarella (page 16), as it is rich and delicious with tomatoes and basil. For meltability, however, this is the one to go with. Use it to make killer pizza, calzones, and lasagne.

meltable MOZZARELLA

MAKES ABOUT 1 POUND

1 cup plain, unsweetened nondairy yogurt (preferably homemade, page 56)

½ cup water

⅓ cup canola oil

2 teaspoons salt

6 tablespoons tapioca flour

1 tablespoon carrageenan powder

½ teaspoon xanthan gum (optional)

8 cups ice water

1. **Process the ingredients.**
Put the yogurt, water, oil, and 1 teaspoon of the salt in a blender. Process until smooth and creamy, occasionally stopping to scrape down the blender jar and move the mixture toward the blades.

2. **Culture the cheese.**
Transfer to a clean glass bowl or container, cover, and let rest at room temperature for 8 to 24 hours, until mildly sharp in flavor.

3. **Thicken the cheese.**
Transfer to a heavy medium saucepan and whisk in the tapioca flour and carrageenan. For a stretchier consistency, whisk in the optional xanthan gum. Cook over medium heat, stirring almost constantly with the whisk, until very smooth, thick, gooey, and glossy, 3 to 5 minutes.

4. **Form the cheese.**
To make a brine, put the ice water and remaining teaspoon of salt in a large bowl and stir until the salt dissolves. Form the cheese into balls using a small ice-cream scoop, dropping them into the brine as you go. They will harden almost instantly. Cover and refrigerate, keeping the cheese stored in the brine.

STORAGE NOTES: Covered and stored in the brine, Meltable Mozzarella will keep for about 1 week in the refrigerator.

Per ounce: calories: 59 protein: 0 g, fat: 5 g, saturated fat: 0 g, carbohydrate: 4 g, sodium: 270 mg, calcium: 21 mg

4

Almost-Instant Cheeses

The recipes in this chapter are for times when you just can't wait a few days for a cultured vegan cheese to age. As explained previously, aging is what allows most of the cheeses in chapters 1 through 3 to develop complex flavors akin to those of dairy cheeses, including sharpness. Because the cheeses in this chapter aren't cultured, they'll lack a certain depth of flavor and may not be quite as convincing in the role of dairy analogs. Still, the cheese alternatives in this chapter are darn tasty, and they'll definitely do the trick when you just can't wait!

This version of ricotta, which can be made in a jiffy, is a fine filling for lasagne, stuffed pasta shells, calzones, and other such dishes. The recipe is for a basic, plain ricotta, but you can enhance it by adding garlic, herbs, and olive oil, as in the variation.

easy TOFU RICOTTA

MAKES ABOUT 2¼ CUPS

1 pound medium-firm regular tofu

¼ cup plain, unsweetened nondairy yogurt (preferably homemade, page 56)

1 tablespoon nutritional yeast flakes

1 teaspoon freshly squeezed lemon juice

½ teaspoon salt

Put all the ingredients in a medium bowl. Mash with a fork until the mixture is thoroughly combined and the tofu is in small bits, similar to the texture of dairy-based ricotta.

STORAGE NOTES: Stored in a covered container in the refrigerator, Easy Tofu Ricotta will keep for about 2 days.

GARLIC-BASIL RICOTTA: For a great pizza topping or filling for ravioli, stir in 3 to 4 cloves of garlic, minced, ½ cup of lightly packed slivered fresh basil leaves, and 3 to 4 tablespoons of extra-virgin olive oil.

Per ½ cup: calories: 124, protein: 13 g, fat: 6 g, saturated fat: 1 g, carbohydrate: 5 g, sodium: 247 mg, calcium: 185 mg

Whether this creamy ricotta is used in lasagne or ravioli, no one would guess that it's made from almonds. It looks amazingly like dairy ricotta and has a similar texture to boot: fluffy with a slight graininess. It's delicious in all sorts of savory dishes and desserts, but I also recommend trying it on its own as a spread for your morning toast with a bit of jam. It's wonderful just like that.

ALMOND ricotta

MAKES ABOUT 4 CUPS

2 cups blanched almonds (see note), soaked in water for 8 to 12 hours and drained

1 cup water

Salt

Put the almonds, water, and a pinch of salt in a blender. Process until light, fluffy, and fairly creamy but not perfectly smooth, occasionally stopping to scrape down the blender jar and move the mixture toward the blades. Taste and stir in more salt if desired.

STORAGE NOTES: Stored in a covered container in the refrigerator, Almond Ricotta will keep for about 1 week.

NOTE: You can also use raw almonds with skins. After soaking, their skins should slip off easily. Simply squeeze one almond at a time between your thumb and index finger. But be careful, or the almonds are likely to shoot across the room! If the skins don't come off easily, pour boiling water over the almonds to cover. Let soak for 1 to 2 minutes, then drain. As soon as they're cool enough to handle, it will be easy to skin them.

Per ½ cup: calories: 218, protein: 8 g, fat: 19 g, saturated fat: 1 g, carbohydrate: 4 g, sodium: 27 mg, calcium: 100 mg

The secret to this rich and creamy tofu ricotta is the addition of a thick cashew cream that's similar to a béchamel sauce. This recipe is easy to put together and works great in any savory dish that calls for ricotta.

GARLIC-BASIL CASHEW ricotta

MAKES ABOUT 2½ CUPS

½ cup raw cashews

½ cup water

1 pound firm regular tofu

¼ cup slivered fresh basil leaves, lightly packed

2 tablespoons nutritional yeast flakes

2 cloves garlic, minced

½ teaspoon salt

Few drops freshly squeezed lemon juice

1. **Make a thick cashew cream.**
Put the cashews and water in a blender. Process until smooth and creamy, occasionally stopping to scrape down the blender jar and move the mixture toward the blades. Transfer to a small heavy saucepan and cook over medium heat, stirring frequently, until the mixture comes to a boil. Decrease the heat to low and cook, stirring constantly, until considerably thickened, about 1 minute.

2. **Mix the ingredients.**
Put the tofu in a medium bowl and mash well with a fork. Add the basil, nutritional yeast, garlic, salt, and lemon juice and mix well. Add the cashew mixture and mix until thoroughly combined.

STORAGE NOTES: Stored in a covered container in the refrigerator, Garlic-Basil Cashew Ricotta will keep for about 3 days.

Per ½ cup: calories: 198, protein: 15 g, fat: 12 g, saturated fat: 2 g, carbohydrate: 9 g, sodium: 224 mg, calcium: 171 mg

This fairly dry, simple cheese can be used in place of ricotta or cottage cheese. It doesn't melt, but it does provide a nice filling for lasagne and other pasta dishes. To use it as a spread for crackers or bread, flavor it with herbs and spices to suit your tastes. The method here is similar to how tofu is usually made: the soy milk is coagulated, then the curds are separated from the liquid. Note that you'll need a kitchen thermometer for this recipe.

FARMER'S cheese

MAKES 2 CUPS

8 cups plain, unsweetened soy milk

6 teaspoons cider vinegar

½ teaspoon salt, plus more as desired

1. Coagulate the soy milk.

Put the soy milk in a large heavy pot and cook, stirring occasionally, until heated to 200 degrees F. Decrease the heat to low and stir in the vinegar, 1 teaspoon at a time. The soy milk will froth and curdle as the vinegar is added, with the curds increasingly separating from the liquid over a 10-minute period.

2. Drain the curds.

Line a sieve or colander with a double layer of cheesecloth, using enough cheesecloth that it hangs over the edges. Put the sieve over a bowl to catch the liquid (see note). Transfer the soy milk curds to the lined sieve and let drain for about 10 minutes. Stir in ½ teaspoon of the salt, then taste and add more salt if desired. Gather the corners of the cheesecloth and tie them in a knot at the top to form a bag. Hang the bag over a bowl (or tie it over the kitchen faucet so the liquid drains in the sink). Let drain for about 1 hour, until firm.

STORAGE NOTES: Stored in a covered container in the refrigerator, Farmer's Cheese will keep for about 2 weeks.

NOTE: Save the liquid and use it for smoothies or soups, or at least to water your plants.

Per ¼ cup calories: 131, protein: 10 g, fat: 4 g, saturated fat: 1 g, carbohydrate: 13 g, sodium: 238 mg, calcium: 80 mg

Here's an almost-instant block of cheese that can be grated, sliced, or melted. Try it with crackers, in sandwiches, or atop nachos. When made without the optional oil, it's a very heart-healthy, low-fat cheese substitute. If fat content isn't a concern, add the oil for a more authentic texture and enjoy a nostalgic taste trip to the days when processed cheese was a staple in many households.

OAT AMERICAN cheese

MAKES ABOUT 2½ CUPS

2½ cups water

1 cup rolled oats

⅔ cup nutritional yeast flakes

¼ cup rejuvelac (preferably homemade, page 6), ¼ cup plain, unsweetened nondairy yogurt (preferably homemade, page 56), or 1 teaspoon freshly squeezed lemon juice

3 tablespoons medium brown miso

½ roasted red bell pepper, skinned and seeded (see sidebar, page 77)

½ teaspoon salt

1 teaspoon prepared mustard

½ cup refined coconut oil or canola oil (optional)

1 tablespoon agar powder, or 3 tablespoons agar flakes (see note)

1 tablespoon carrageenan powder

1. **Cook the oats.**

Put the water and oats in a heavy medium saucepan and bring to a boil over medium-high heat. Decrease the heat to medium-low and simmer, stirring frequently, until thick, about 5 minutes.

2. **Process the ingredients.**

Transfer to a blender. Add the nutritional yeast, rejuvelac, miso, bell pepper, salt, mustard, and optional oil as desired for a richer-tasting cheese. Process until smooth and creamy.

3. **Thicken the cheese.**

Transfer to a heavy medium saucepan and whisk in the agar and carrageenan. Cook over medium heat, stirring frequently with the whisk, until thick, 4 to 5 minutes.

4. **Form the cheese.**

Pour the mixture into a glass or nonreactive metal mold and smooth the top. Cover and let cool completely at room temperature. Refrigerate for at least 6 hours, until firm.

STORAGE NOTES: Wrapped in plastic wrap and stored in a ziplock bag, Oat American Cheese will keep for about 2 weeks in the refrigerator or 4 months in the freezer.

NOTE: The amount of agar in this recipe creates a sliceable but soft cheese; for a firmer consistency, increase the amount of agar. Using 2 tablespoons of agar powder or 6 tablespoons of agar flakes will yield a very firm consistency similar to traditional Cheddar.

Per ¼ cup: calories: 89, protein: 8 g, fat: 2 g, saturated fat: 0 g, carbohydrate: 11 g, sodium: 307 mg, calcium: 11 mg

This fairly firm cheese with a hint of smokiness slices beautifully. For a fabulous sandwich, slice a baguette lengthwise and stuff it with grilled veggies and this cheese. It's also great in a grilled cheese sandwich with veggie sausage on the side.

smoked PROVOLONE

MAKES ABOUT 1 POUND

1 cup plain, unsweetened nondairy yogurt (preferably homemade, page 56)

½ cup rejuvelac (preferably homemade, page 6)

⅓ cup canola oil

⅓ cup pine nuts

¼ cup nutritional yeast flakes

¼ cup tapioca flour

1 tablespoon carrageenan powder, or 2 tablespoons agar powder

1 teaspoon salt

½ teaspoon liquid smoke (see note)

1. **Process the ingredients.**
Put all the ingredients in a blender. Process until smooth and creamy.

2. **Cook the mixture.**
Pour the mixture into a heavy medium saucepan. Cook over medium heat, stirring almost constantly with a wooden spoon. The mixture will be very lumpy at first. Once it's smooth, decrease the heat to low and simmer, stirring occasionally, for about 2 minutes.

3. **Form the cheese.**
Pour the mixture into a glass or nonreactive metal mold and smooth the top. Cover and let cool to room temperature. Refrigerate for at least 3 hours, until firm.

STORAGE NOTES: Wrapped in plastic wrap and stored in a ziplock bag, Smoked Provolone will keep for about 6 weeks in the refrigerator or 4 months in the freezer.

AIR-DRIED SMOKED PROVOLONE: This cheese will develop a sharper flavor if air-dried. To air-dry it, remove the cheese from the mold once it's firm and sprinkle about ¼ teaspoon of salt evenly over the entire surface. Put the cheese on a drying rack in a cool place with good air circulation and let air-dry for 2 to 3 days.

NOTE: Strange as it may sound, liquid smoke is exactly that: smoke that has been condensed, collected, and packaged in little bottles, generally with no additives. It is sold in the condiment section of most grocery stores.

Per ounce: calories: 91, protein: 2 g, fat: 7 g, saturated fat: 1 g, carbohydrate: 5 g, sodium: 138 mg, calcium: 11 mg

It hardly takes a minute to make this Parmesan substitute, yet the result is a great condiment that will keep for weeks in the refrigerator. I like to sprinkle it on salads, pastas, and cooked veggies.

nut **PARMESAN**

MAKES ABOUT 1½ CUPS

1 cup pine nuts, almonds, or walnuts (see note)

1 cup nutritional yeast flakes

½ teaspoon salt

Put all the ingredients in a food processor. Process until the ingredients are thoroughly combined and the texture is granular.

STORAGE NOTES: Stored in a covered container in the refrigerator, Nut Parmesan will keep for 6 to 8 weeks.

NOTE: Different nuts yield different flavors. My favorite is pine nuts, but almonds and walnuts are also good. When using walnuts, take care not to overprocess or you'll end up with nut butter.

Per 2 tablespoons: calories: 143, protein: 9 g, fat: 10 g, saturated fat: 1 g, carbohydrate: 7 g, sodium: 94 mg, calcium: 2 mg

CHAPTER

Other Dairy Alternatives

If you miss cheese, you probably miss other dairy products too. There are many recipes for nut-based nondairy milks in cookbooks and online, so here I just provide an innovative version that's extremely quick and easy because it uses almond butter, not raw, soaked nuts. This chapter also includes recipes that allow you to replicate sour cream, crème fraîche, yogurt, and whipped cream in your home kitchen using only wholesome natural foods, without highly processed ingredients such as soy protein isolates, which are found in so many store-bought vegan analogs of dairy products. All of the recipes in this chapter are easy to make and require only a few ingredients—and in a couple of cases, a little patience. The rich, creamy flavors of these alternatives will add new dimensions to your meals without all of the cholesterol of their dairy counterparts.

I've been making almond milk from raw almonds for years and still do, but I was delighted to discover that it can be made quickly and easily using almond butter. The beauty of this method is that you can make almond milk in just about any blender, and there's no need to strain the milk through a sieve or nut milk bag. Just twenty seconds of blending and—voilà!—delicious, creamy almond milk.

ALMOND milk

MAKES ABOUT 3 CUPS

3 cups water

1 to 2 tablespoons almond butter

Put the water and almond butter in a blender, using 1 tablespoon of almond butter for a light version and up to 2 tablespoons for a richer flavor. Process until white, milky, and completely smooth.

STORAGE NOTES: Stored in a sealed glass jar in the refrigerator, Almond Milk will keep for about 5 days.

Per cup: calories: 45, protein: 2 g, fat: 4 g, saturated fat: 0 g, carbohydrate: 1 g, sodium: 9 mg, calcium: 10 mg

Caprese Salad, *page 67*

nachos with Low-Fat Chipotle Cheese Sauce, *page 63*

This versatile, all-purpose substitute for heavy cream will enrich salad dressings, sauces, soups, and other dishes. You can make any quantity you like; just use a three-to-one ratio of water to cashews.

CASHEW cream

MAKES ABOUT 3½ CUPS

3 cups water

1 cup raw cashews, soaked for 3 to 8 hours and drained (see note)

Put the water and cashews in a blender. Process until smooth and creamy. If not using immediately, transfer to a storage container, cover, and refrigerate for no more than 12 hours.

STORAGE NOTES: Cashew Cream is best used the day it's made, as it can separate and become gooey.

NOTE: If you are using a high-speed blender, it isn't necessary to soak the cashews.

Per ½ cup: calories: 120, protein: 4g, fat: 10 g, saturated fat: 2 g, carbohydrate: 6 g, sodium: 3 mg, calcium: 8 mg

Blending cashews with soy milk prior to culturing results in a flavorful, rich yogurt. Enjoy the yogurt as is, or use it to make Basic Yogurt Cheese (page 22), which can be flavored a number of ways. The yogurt can also be used as part of the base for Sour Cream (page 58) and several of the cheese recipes in this book, including all of the meltable cheeses in chapter 3.

cashew YOGURT

MAKES ABOUT 5 CUPS

4 cups plain or vanilla soy milk or almond milk (use plain if the yogurt will serve as the base for cheese)

⅔ cup raw cashews, soaked in water for 3 hours and drained

3 tablespoons plain, unsweetened nondairy yogurt

1. **Process the ingredients.**
   Put 1 cup of the soy milk and the cashews in a blender and process until smooth and creamy.

2. **Heat the soy milk.**
   Transfer to a heavy medium saucepan and stir in the remaining 3 cups of soy milk with a whisk. Warm over low heat, whisking occasionally, until the mixture reaches 110 degrees F or until a few drops placed on your wrist feel slightly warm. Remove from the heat.

3. **Culture the yogurt.**
   Add the nondairy yogurt and stir until thoroughly combined. Pour into a clean 1-quart glass jar and cover. Let rest in a warm place for 4 to 8 hours, until set and the desired degree of tartness has been achieved. Refrigerate the yogurt; it will thicken even more as it cools.

STORAGE NOTES: Stored in a covered container in the refrigerator, Cashew Yogurt will keep for 1 to 2 weeks.

NOTES: The idea of making homemade yogurt without using a yogurt maker may seem daunting, but keep in mind that humans have been making yogurt for thousands of years without any special equipment. Once you understand a few simple principles and rules, you'll find it's easy to do. The only "special" equipment you might want to invest in is an inexpensive kitchen thermometer.

Per cup: calories: 221, protein: 12 g, fat: 12 g, saturated fat: 2 g, carbohydrate: 17 g, sodium: 88 mg, calcium: 83 mg

- The milk must be warm to promote the growth of the bacterial culture, but if it is too hot, it can kill the culture. The temperature should be about 110 degrees F. You can test the temperature by placing a few drops of the milk on your wrist—if it feels warm but not hot, it's ready. Alternatively, you can use a kitchen thermometer.

- Use only clean glass jars for culturing yogurt.

- Culture the yogurt in a warm place. If you can set the oven as low as 110 degrees F, use that. On a warm, sunny day, it is often enough to wrap the jar in a couple of layers of towels and set it outside in the sun. Other options are a warm corner of the kitchen or in front of a sunny window.

- The yogurt should set up in 4 to 6 hours, although it could take as long as 8 hours, depending on the ambient temperature. The longer it is allowed to set, the more tangy and tart it will become. For a sweeter, more delicate flavor, culture just until thickened and set; for a tangier flavor, culture for a full 6 to 8 hours.

- Yogurt will separate if cultured at too high a temperature or for too long, so don't exceed 110 degrees F, and refrigerate it once it has set. If it does separate, don't despair; just use the recipe for Basic Yogurt Cheese (page 22) to thicken it and make cheese.

- Always reserve 2 to 3 tablespoons of each batch of yogurt for culturing the next batch.

With just three ingredients and a bit of patience, you can make a rich, creamy, thick vegan sour cream that can be used in any recipe that calls for the dairy-based version.

SOUR cream

MAKES ABOUT 1¼ CUPS

1 cup raw cashews, soaked in water for 3 to 8 hours and drained

1 cup rejuvelac (preferably homemade, page 6)

Pinch salt

1. Process the ingredients.

Put the cashews, rejuvelac, and salt in a blender. Process until smooth and creamy, occasionally stopping to scrape down the blender jar and move the mixture toward the blades.

2. Culture the sour cream.

Transfer the mixture to a clean glass bowl or container, cover, and let rest at room temperature for 24 to 48 hours, until a bit thicker and pleasantly sour.

3. Thicken the sour cream.

Line a sieve or colander with a double layer of cheesecloth. Put the sieve over a bowl and pour in the sour cream. Let drain for at least 3 hours, until thick. Discard the liquid. Transfer to a container, cover, and refrigerate. The sour cream will continue to thicken as it chills.

STORAGE NOTES: Stored in a covered container in the refrigerator, Sour Cream will keep for about 2 weeks.

VARIATION: Replace the rejuvelac with ¾ cup water plus ¼ cup plain, unsweetened nondairy yogurt (preferably homemade, page 56).

CRÈME FRAÎCHE: Put 1 to 1¼ cups of Sour Cream and ½ cup of silken tofu in a blender and process until smooth and creamy. Transfer to a container, cover, and refrigerate for at least 3 hours, until thick.

Per ¼ cup: calories: 172, protein: 6 g, fat: 13 g, saturated fat: 2 g, carbohydrate: 8 g, sodium: 48 mg, calcium: 11 mg

Because the creamy component of coconut milk is high in saturated fat, it can be whipped just like heavy whipping cream, complete with the light, fluffy, and oh-so-rich texture and mouthfeel of whipped cream. If you want to mask the coconut flavor, good-quality vanilla extract will do the trick, as in this recipe, or you might add a little brandy. While it is delectably vegan, it's still high in fat and calories, so you may want to save it for special occasions. Be forewarned that you can't use light coconut milk for this recipe, and that you'll need to refrigerate the coconut milk in the cans for at least twenty-four hours for the magic to happen.

fluffy whipped COCONUT CREAM

MAKES ABOUT 4 CUPS

1¼ cups chilled coconut cream
(see note)

2 teaspoons vanilla extract, plus more
as desired

2 tablespoons agave nectar,
or 3 tablespoons powdered sugar,
plus more as desired

Using a handheld mixer or a stand mixer fitted with the whisk attachment, beat the coconut cream until light and fluffy. Add the vanilla extract and agave nectar and beat until soft peaks form. Taste and add more vanilla extract or agave nectar if desired.

STORAGE NOTES: Unlike its dairy-based counterpart, Fluffy Whipped Coconut Cream will keep for 2 to 3 days in the refrigerator.

NOTE: To make the coconut cream, refrigerate 2 cans (about 14 ounces each) of regular coconut milk (not the light variety) for at least 24 hours. Different brands of coconut milk, and even different cans, will contain varying amounts of fat. After refrigerating cans of coconut milk, I've found some with only one-third of the volume solidified, whereas in other cases almost the entire can is solid, so it isn't possible to specify a precise number of cans of coconut milk to use. When you're ready to make the coconut cream, open the *bottom* of one can of coconut milk and drain off the liquid. (Reserve the liquid for another use, such as in smoothies, in curries, or as the liquid in baked goods.) Measure the solidified portion; you may have enough without having to open the second can.

Per ½ cup: calories: 142, protein: 1 g, fat: 13 g, saturated fat: 12 g, carbohydrate: 6 g, sodium: 2 mg, calcium: 4 mg

Cheese Sauces and Fondue

Given that you're reading this book and making vegan cheeses, you undoubtedly enjoy rich, complex flavors. These same flavor qualities are what make vegan cheese a great addition to savory dishes, providing depth, tang, and character. Of course, another way to ramp up the flavor is to apply a cheesy sauce to main dishes and vegetables. All of the recipes in this chapter can be made very quickly, giving you even more almost-instant vegan cheese options beyond the recipes in chapter 4.

As you might guess from the name, this recipe doesn't have the character of any particular type of cheese; it's just a thick, cheesy concoction that can be poured over polenta, cooked potatoes or broccoli, or any food that is enhanced by a cheese sauce. If using it as a sauce, you'll probably want to omit the xanthan gum. For a stretchier consistency, add some or all of the xanthan gum, which will also thicken the sauce, allowing it to be used more like a cheese—for example, as a topping for pizza. If you like, culture the cashew cream before seasoning and heating the sauce; this will create a sharp flavor with more depth.

EASY CHEESY sauce

MAKES ABOUT 2½ CUPS

2½ cups water

1 cup raw cashews

¼ cup nutritional yeast flakes

1 teaspoon salt

1 to 3 teaspoons freshly squeezed lemon juice (optional)

½ to 1 teaspoon xanthan gum (optional)

1. **Make the cashew cream.**

   Put the water and cashews in a blender, and process until smooth and creamy.

2. **Culture the cashew cream (optional).**

   Transfer to a clean glass bowl or container, cover, and let rest at room temperature for 8 to 24 hours, until the cashew cream has a deep, sharp flavor.

3. **Season and thicken the sauce.**

   Transfer to a heavy medium saucepan and whisk in the nutritional yeast, salt, and 1 teaspoon of the optional lemon juice. Cook over medium heat, stirring almost constantly with the whisk, until very thick, 3 to 4 minutes. For a stretchier consistency, whisk in the optional xanthan gum; the more of the xanthan gum you use, the stretchier and gooier the sauce will be. Cook, stirring constantly with the whisk, for 1 minute. Taste and add more lemon juice if desired.

   STORAGE NOTES: Stored in a covered container in the refrigerator, Easy Cheesy Sauce will keep for about 4 days.

Per ½ cup: calories: 200, protein: 10 g, fat: 14 g, saturated fat: 2 g, carbohydrate: 12 g, sodium: 433 mg, calcium: 12 mg

It's hard to believe that a recipe that can be whipped up in a matter of minutes, like this one, can be so good! Of course, this rich and creamy sauce is perfect for fettuccine, perhaps with some veggies thrown in, such as fresh baby spinach, sautéed red bell peppers or broccoli, or grilled or roasted portobello mushrooms or butternut squash. But don't stop there. This sauce is versatile and lends itself to casseroles, lasagne and even pizza.

rich and creamy ALFREDO SAUCE

MAKES ABOUT 4 CUPS (ENOUGH FOR ABOUT 1 POUND OF PASTA)

3½ to 4 cups water

1½ cups raw cashews

½ cup dry white wine

⅓ to ½ cup nutritional yeast flakes

4 to 6 cloves garlic, minced

1 teaspoon salt

Ground pepper

1. **Make the cashew cream.**
   Put the water and cashews in a blender, and process until smooth and creamy.

2. **Season and thicken the sauce.**
   Pour into a large heavy skillet or medium saucepan and bring to a simmer over low heat. Stir in the wine, ⅓ cup of the nutritional yeast, 4 cloves of the garlic, and the salt with a wooden spoon. Cook, stirring frequently, until thick, 3 to 5 minutes. Season with pepper to taste and add more nutritional yeast (for a cheesier flavor) or garlic if desired. If the sauce gets too thick, stir in a bit of water to achieve the desired consistency.

STORAGE NOTES: Stored in a covered container in the refrigerator, Rich and Creamy Alfredo Sauce will keep for about 2 days.

Per ½ cup: calories: 203, protein: 10 g, fat: 13 g, saturated fat: 2 g, carbohydrate: 12 g, sodium: 274 mg, calcium: 15 mg

You won't have to feel guilty about eating nachos when you use this sauce, which is delectably creamy and gooey but low in fat. Plus, there's no need to bake or broil the nachos; just pour the sauce right over the chips and serve. The chipotle in adobo sauce adds a wonderful smokiness that's balanced nicely by the sweetness of the butternut squash. Depending on how you handle the heat, you can use more or less of the chile. Serve salsa and guacamole alongside your nachos and have a fiesta! If you have any of this sauce left over, try using it to make a quick macaroni and cheese or add it to marinara for a cheesy pasta sauce.

LOW-FAT CHIPOTLE cheese sauce

See photo facing page 55.

MAKES ABOUT 3 CUPS

1 cup cooked and mashed butternut squash

¾ cup plain, unsweetened nondairy yogurt (preferably homemade, page 56)

¾ cup water

½ onion, quartered

5 tablespoons nutritional yeast flakes

¼ cup raw cashews

3 tablespoons tapioca flour

½ chipotle chile in adobo sauce, plus more as desired

1 teaspoon salt

1. Process the ingredients.

Put all the ingredients in a blender. Process until smooth and creamy, occasionally stopping to scrape down the blender jar and move the mixture toward the blades.

2. Thicken the sauce.

Transfer to a heavy medium saucepan. Cook over medium heat, stirring frequently with a wooden spoon, until thick and gooey, 2 to 5 minutes. Taste, and if you'd like it a little hotter, mince more chipotle chile and stir it in.

STORAGE NOTES: Stored in a covered container in the refrigerator, Low-Fat Chipotle Cheese Sauce will keep for about 4 days.

Per ¼ cup: calories: 59, protein: 3 g, fat: 2 g, saturated fat: 0 g, carbohydrate: 8 g, sodium: 182 mg, calcium: 17 mg

This is a wonderful sauce for pouring over steamed broccoli, baked potatoes, or even a steamed whole head of cauliflower. Or for easy mac and cheese, mix it with cooked pasta. If you have any left over, it makes a great spread for sandwiches once it's chilled, or reheat it and toss it with veggies.

creamy CHEDDAR SAUCE

MAKES ABOUT 3½ CUPS

3 cups water

¾ cup raw cashews

1 cup Sharp Cheddar (page 14), grated or in chunks, plus more as desired

2 to 3 tablespoons nutritional yeast flakes

Salt

Ground pepper

1. **Make the cashew milk.**
Put the water and cashews in a blender, and process until smooth and creamy.

2. **Cook the sauce.**
Pour into a heavy medium saucepan. Cook over medium heat, stirring occasionally, until hot but not bubbling. Add the cheese and 2 tablespoons of the nutritional yeast and cook, stirring often with a wire whisk, until the cheese is completely melted, about 5 minutes. Season with salt and pepper to taste. Stir in more Cheddar or nutritional yeast as desired for a cheesier flavor.

STORAGE NOTES: Stored in a covered container in the refrigerator, Creamy Cheddar Sauce will keep for about 2 days.

Per ½ cup: calories: 167, protein: 7 g, fat: 12 g, saturated fat: 2 g, carbohydrate: 10 g, sodium: 117 mg, calcium: 11 mg

This is a rich, creamy, and wickedly delicious concoction. Warm cubes of French bread are traditional for dipping, but I recommend also including an assortment of vegetables for added flavor, color, and nutrition. If using baby potatoes, steam or roast them first. As for other veggies, try steamed cauliflower or broccoli florets or green beans, or sautéed or grilled mushrooms. If the mushrooms are small, use them whole or halved cut larger mushrooms into large chunks. Although a fondue pot is ideal for keeping the fondue hot at the table, a double boiler with very hot water in the lower pot also works well.

cheese FONDUE

MAKES 4 TO 6 SERVINGS AS AN ENTRÉE, OR 8 TO 12 SERVINGS AS AN APPETIZER

1 pound **Soft Gruyère** (page 13), **made through step 1** (no need to let it culture), **or Hard Gruyère** (page 13)

1 cup dry white wine, plus more as needed

¼ cup water, plus more as needed

3 tablespoons tapioca flour

1. **Melt the cheese.**

   If making Soft Gruyère specifically for the fondue, at the end of step 1 leave the cheese in the blender, add the wine, and process until thoroughly blended. Transfer to a fondue pot or the top of a double boiler. If using cheese made in advance, cut it into ½-inch chunks, put it in the fondue pot or double boiler, and add the wine.

2. **Heat the mixture.**

   Over the flame of a fondue pot or in the double boiler on the stovetop, gently heat the mixture, stirring frequently, until hot but not bubbling, about 5 minutes; if using Hard Gruyère, cook until the cheese is completely melted. If the mixture becomes lumpy, whisk until smooth.

3. **Thicken the fondue.**

   Combine the water and tapioca flour in a small bowl and stir to form a smooth paste. Add to the cheese mixture and cook, stirring frequently, until the fondue thickens and becomes a bit stretchy, 2 to 3 minutes. If the fondue gets too thick, whisk in a bit more wine or water to achieve the desired consistency. Serve immediately.

   STORAGE NOTES: Stored in a covered container in the refrigerator, leftover Cheese Fondue will keep for about 2 days.

   SWISS CHEESE SAUCE: Any leftover fondue can be used to make a tasty cheese sauce for pasta or vegetables. Just warm the fondue and stir in water or plain, unsweetened nondairy milk to achieve the desired consistency. Pour over pasta, a baked potato, or other vegetables and enjoy!

Per serving (based on 5 servings): calories: 451, protein: 11 g, fat: 33 g, saturated fat: 12g, carbohydrate: 22 g, sodium: 542 mg, calcium: 24 mg

7

First Courses and Small Plates

Once you've mastered the art of making vegan cheeses, you can begin to use your creations in all sorts of recipes. The fun begins here, with appetizers. Whether it's a Caprese Salad (page 67) that will transport you to Tuscany or luxurious Artichokes Stuffed with Almonds and Cheese (page 82), these cheese-laced—or downright cheese-filled—recipes will get your meal started on the right note. And then you just keep on going . .

Featuring the colors of the Italian flag—red, green, and white—this salad is as beautiful as it is delicious. Slices of ripe tomato alternate with creamy Fresh Mozzarella and fresh basil leaves, and balsamic vinegar and extra-virgin olive oil are drizzled over the top. It doesn't get any easier—or any better! When this salad is sandwiched between two slices of bread, it becomes a caprese sandwich; try it with a little pesto spread on the bread.

CAPRESE salad

See photo facing page 54.

MAKES ABOUT 6 SERVINGS

3 to 4 ripe tomatoes

1 pound Fresh Mozzarella (page 16)

1 cup fresh basil leaves, lightly packed

Balsamic vinegar, for drizzling

Extra-virgin olive oil (optional), for drizzling

Salt

1. **Slice the cheese and tomatoes and assemble.**

   Slice the tomatoes and cheese into rounds, between ¼ and ½ inch thick. On a platter, arrange the tomatoes, cheese, and basil in a circle or spiral, overlapping them as you go.

2. **Dress the salad.**

   Drizzle a little vinegar and optional oil over the top, then sprinkle with a little salt. Serve immediately.

Per serving: calories: 326, protein: 11 g, fat: 24 g, saturated fat: 4 g, carbohydrate: 19 g, sodium: 78 mg, calcium: 47 mg

This healthful dip is so rich and delicious that it rivals traditional sour cream–based offerings—with the bonus that it isn't laden with calories and fat. It's a wonderful accompaniment to crudités. If you like, serve it in a bread bowl. Even teens will enjoy it.

spinach and roasted RED BELL PEPPER DIP

MAKES ABOUT 3 CUPS

3 tablespoons water

1 onion, diced

1 bunch spinach (about 1 pound), trimmed and coarsely chopped

1 cup Cashew Cream Cheese (page 20)

1 roasted red bell pepper (see sidebar, page 77), skinned and seeded

¼ cup fresh basil leaves, lightly packed

2 tablespoons freshly squeezed lemon juice

1 clove garlic

Salt

Ground pepper

1. **Prepare the vegetables.**

Combine the water and onion in a large skillet over low heat. Cook, stirring occasionally, until the onion is golden and very tender, about 20 minutes. Transfer to a food processor. In the same skillet, cook the spinach over high heat until wilted, about 4 minutes. Drain in a sieve or colander, then use your hands to squeeze out as much liquid as possible. Put the spinach in the food processor.

2. **Process the ingredients.**

Add the cheese, bell pepper, basil, lemon juice, and garlic and process until fairly smooth but some texture still remains. Season with salt and pepper to taste. Serve immediately or cover, refrigerate, and serve chilled.

Per ¼ cup: calories: 87, protein: 4 g, fat: 6 g, saturated fat: 1 g, carbohydrate: 6 g, sodium: 38 mg, calcium: 49 mg

This appetizer is so simple and yet so elegant—and one of the reasons you want to have some Cashew Chèvre on hand whenever fresh figs are in season. You never know when company might show up on your doorstep! You can use any type of fresh figs here—black Mission, brown, green—all are delicious.

figs stuffed with LEMON-SCENTED CHÈVRE

MAKES ABOUT 8 SERVINGS

1 cup Cashew Chèvre (page 8)
or Basic Cashew Cheese (page 7)

1 teaspoon grated lemon zest

1 teaspoon freshly squeezed
lemon juice

Pinch salt

8 to 10 large, ripe fresh figs, halved
lengthwise

¼ cup walnuts, lightly toasted
(see note) and finely chopped

1 tablespoon agave nectar

1. **Season the cheese.**
Put the cheese, lemon zest and juice, and salt in a small bowl. Mix well.

2. **Stuff the figs.**
Mound a tablespoon of the cheese atop each fig half. Sprinkle the walnuts evenly over the cheese and drizzle with the agave nectar. Serve immediately.

STUFFED FIGS WITH BALSAMIC REDUCTION: Instead of stuffing the figs with the cheese mixture, use plain Cashew Chèvre. Omit the walnuts and agave nectar. Instead, drizzle a balsamic reduction over the stuffed figs. To make the reduction, put 1 cup of balsamic vinegar in a small heavy saucepan. Bring to a boil over medium-high heat, then decrease the heat to medium-low and simmer, stirring occasionally, until reduced to about ¼ cup of thick, syrupy liquid, about 20 minutes.

NOTE: To toast walnuts, preheat the oven to 325 degrees F. Spread the walnuts in a single layer on a baking sheet or in a baking pan. Bake for 5 to 10 minutes, stirring or shaking the pan once or twice, until lightly browned and fragrant.

Per serving: calories: 130, protein: 3 g, fat: 7 g, saturated fat: 1 g, carbohydrate: 15 g, sodium: 62 mg, calcium: 27 mg

Highly versatile Soft Gruyère is the star of this easy appetizer with a sophisticated flavor. You can make the red wine glaze up to the point of thickening as far as one week in advance and refrigerate it until you assemble the croustades; simply reheat it in a small saucepan and stir in the arrowroot starch while the croustades bake.

GRUYÈRE AND PEAR croustades with red wine glaze

MAKES ABOUT 8 SERVINGS

GLAZE

1½ cups robust, dry red wine (such as Cabernet Sauvignon or Zinfandel)

2 to 3 tablespoon agave nectar or sugar

3 sprigs fresh thyme

¼ teaspoon salt

1 tablespoon water

1 to 2 teaspoons arrowroot starch

CROUSTADES

2 firm but ripe pears

½ baguette

1½ cups Soft Gruyère (page 13)

1. **Make the glaze.**

Combine the wine, 2 tablespoons of the agave nectar, and the thyme and salt in a heavy medium saucepan. Bring to a simmer over medium heat. Decrease the heat to medium-low and simmer, stirring occasionally, until reduced to about ½ cup of thick, syrupy liquid, about 20 minutes. Remove the thyme. (If not assembling the croustades right away, let cool to room temperature, then store in a covered container in the refrigerator for up to 1 week. Reheat before using.) Combine the water and arrowroot and stir to form a smooth paste. While the wine mixture is hot, add the arrowroot paste and cook, stirring occasionally, over medium heat until the glaze is no longer cloudy, thickens slightly, and is glossy, 30 to 60 seconds. Taste and stir in more agave nectar if desired.

2. **Assemble and bake.**

Preheat the oven to 400 degrees F. Slice the pears lengthwise into 16 equal pieces. Slice the baguette into 16 equal pieces. Spread about 1 rounded tablespoon of the Gruyère on each baguette slice. Top with a slice of pear. Put the croustades on a baking sheet and bake for about 8 minutes, until the edges of the cheese have begun to brown slightly.

3. **Apply the glaze and serve.**

Drizzle about 1 teaspoon of the glaze over each of the croustades and serve immediately.

Per serving: calories: 253, protein: 6 g, fat: 8 g, saturated fat: 3 g, carbohydrate: 30 g, sodium: 378 mg, calcium: 11 mg

Hearty, savory, redolent of herbs and garlic—and, dare I say, meaty—these mushrooms are perfect on a cold night. Stuff button mushrooms and serve them as an appetizer, or stuff large portobellos and serve them as an entrée.

italian STUFFED MUSHROOMS

MAKES 24 STUFFED BUTTON MUSHROOMS, OR
4 TO 6 STUFFED PORTOBELLO MUSHROOMS

24 medium to large button or cremini mushrooms, or 4 to 6 portobello mushrooms

1 teaspoon extra-virgin olive oil, plus more as needed

3 shallots, finely chopped

8 ounces seitan, coarsely chopped

4 ounces Air-Dried Parmesan (page 34) or Sharp Cheddar (page 14), in chunks

2 tablespoons tomato paste

2 cloves garlic, coarsely chopped, plus more as desired

3 to 4 fresh basil leaves, slivered, or ½ teaspoon dried basil

½ teaspoon dried sage

Salt

Ground pepper

1. **Preheat the oven and prepare the baking sheet.**
   Preheat the oven to 350 degrees F. Line a baking sheet with parchment paper.

2. **Cook the mushroom stems and shallots for the filling.**
   Remove and finely chop the mushroom stems. Heat the oil in a large skillet over medium-high heat. Add the shallots and mushroom stems and cook, stirring frequently, until browned, about 8 minutes, adding a bit more oil if needed to prevent sticking.

3. **Make the filling.**
   Put the seitan, cheese, tomato paste, garlic, basil, and sage in a food processor. Pulse until crumbly. Transfer to a bowl. Add the mushroom stems and shallots and mix well with a wooden spoon or your hands. Taste and add more garlic if desired. Season with salt and pepper to taste.

4. **Stuff and bake the mushrooms.**
   Put the mushroom caps on the lined baking sheet, stem-side up. Divide the filling evenly among the mushrooms, slightly mounding it atop each. Bake stuffed button mushrooms for 12 to 15 minutes and stuffed portobellos for 20 minutes, until browned. Serve hot.

Per mushroom: calories: 67, protein: 9 g, fat: 1 g, saturated fat: 0 g, carbohydrate: 5 g, sodium: 80 mg, calcium: 50 mg

If you grow any kind of squash in your garden, from summer to early fall you will have an endless source of blossoms for this superb, delicately flavored appetizer. Upscale grocers and farmers' markets are other good sources for squash blossoms. In this classic Italian dish, the blossoms are usually stuffed with mozzarella or ricotta cheese. Here, light but rich ricotta made from macadamia nuts does the trick.

When picking blossoms, note that the female flowers bloom at the ends of the baby squash, while the male flowers bloom from the stem. You can use both in this dish, but if you pick the female flowers, harvest

stuffed SQUASH BLOSSOMS

MAKES 4 TO 6 SERVINGS

FILLING

1 cup Macadamia Ricotta (page 19)

¼ cup water

2 tablespoons slivered fresh
basil leaves

2 tablespoons minced fresh tarragon

1 clove garlic, minced

Salt

Ground pepper

BLOSSOMS, OIL, AND BATTER

8 to 12 zucchini or squash blossoms

Canola or grapeseed oil, for frying
(3 to 4 cups, depending on the size of
the pot)

1 cup unbleached cake flour or
pastry flour

⅛ teaspoon baking soda

1 to 1¼ cups chilled dry white wine
or water

Salt (optional)

1. **Make the filling.**
Put the ricotta and water in a small bowl and mix well. The consistency will be very soft. Stir in the basil, tarragon, and garlic and season with salt and pepper to taste.

2. **Stuff the blossoms.**
The blossoms can be stuffed up to 30 minutes before frying. Gently pry open the petals if necessary. Using a small spoon, stuff each blossom with about 2 tablespoons of filling; alternatively, use a pastry bag to pipe in the filling. Fill each blossom only about half full. Gently press the petals closed.

3. **Heat the oil.**
Pour oil into a wok or wide pot to a depth of about 2 inches. Put the wok over medium heat.

4. **Mix the batter.**
Put the flour and baking soda in a medium bowl and mix well. Stir in 1 cup of the wine with a fork or whisk just until combined; don't overmix. The batter should be runny and just thick enough to coat the back of a wooden spoon. If it's too thick, add the remaining ¼ cup of wine, 1 tablespoon at a time, to achieve the correct consistency, again being careful not to overmix.

Per serving (based on 5 servings): calories: 504, protein: 4 g, fat: 41 g, saturated fat: 4 g, carbohydrate: 21 g, sodium: 64 mg, calcium: 18 mg

the entire, intact flower and baby squash, which can then be fried together, or roasted as described in the variation. It's easier to stuff the flowers if you harvest them in the morning, when they are open. In the afternoon they tend to close, and then you'll have to pry them apart ever so gently in order to stuff them. You can pick them up to three days in advance of making this dish, although you will have to store them carefully: sprinkle them with water, then wrap gently in a paper towel and store in a plastic bag in the refrigerator.

5. **Check the oil temperature.**

When the oil reaches about 375 degrees F, it's ready. If you don't have a kitchen thermometer, test the oil temperature by adding a drop of the batter to it. If it sinks but rises quickly and steadily to the top, the oil is hot enough. If it sinks to the bottom and lingers there for a moment, the oil isn't yet hot enough. Having the oil at the right temperature is important to achieving a light, crispy texture.

6. **Dip and fry.**

Once the oil is ready, dip a zucchini blossom in the batter, then let the excess batter drip off. Carefully lower the blossom into the oil and cook, carefully turning once, until golden brown, about 2 minutes. Keep adding squash blossoms, but don't overcrowd the pot. The blossoms shouldn't touch each other. Drain briefly on paper towels. Serve immediately, cut in half lengthwise if you like, and sprinkled with salt if desired.

ROASTED BABY ZUCCHINI WITH BLOSSOMS: If you can get baby zucchini with the blossoms attached, you can roast them instead of frying. Preheat the oven to 425 degrees F. Stuff the blossoms with the filling as directed above. Omit the batter, and instead lightly coat the baby zucchini with olive oil, then sprinkle with salt and pepper. Bake for 15 to 20 minutes, until the zucchini are tender and slightly shriveled. Serve topped with a bit of marinara sauce or vegan pesto.

Admittedly, these savory treats are deep-fried, but as a result, they are oh so crispy on the outside and wonderfully soft and creamy on the inside. It's a delightful way to use up any extra cheese you may have in the refrigerator. To create that enticing crunchy coating, you'll need a three-dip frying station with a bowl of seasoned flour, a bowl of egg replacer mixture, and a bowl of panko (Japanese breadcrumbs). If you don't have one of the seasonings for the flour mixture, don't worry; the results will still be delicious.

DEEP-FRIED cheese

MAKES 8 SERVINGS

DIPPING COMPONENTS

1 cup unbleached flour or whole wheat pastry flour

1 tablespoon nutritional yeast flakes

1 teaspoon dried basil

1 teaspoon dried oregano

½ teaspoon granulated garlic

¼ teaspoon salt

⅓ cup water, plus more if needed

¼ cup Ener-G egg replacer (see page 134)

2 cups panko

OIL, CHEESE, AND SAUCE

Canola or grapeseed oil, for frying (3 to 4 cups, depending on the size of the pot)

1 pound Fresh Mozzarella (page 16), Meltable Mozzarella (page 44), or Meltable Muenster (page 41), cut into ¾-inch to 1-inch chunks

2 cups marinara sauce, warmed, for dipping

1. **Set up the dipping components.**

To set up a three-dip fry station, first combine the flour, nutritional yeast, basil, oregano, granulated garlic, and salt in a small bowl. Stir with a whisk until well combined. Put the water and egg replacer in a second small bowl and whisk vigorously until frothy and thick. The consistency should be thick enough to cling to the cheese after it's been dipped in the flour mixture. If it gets too thick as it sits, whisk in up to 2 tablespoons more water. Put the panko in a third small bowl.

2. **Heat the oil.**

Pour oil into a wok or wide pot to a depth of about 2 inches. Put the wok over medium heat.

3. **Coat the cheese.**

Roll a chunk of cheese in the flour mixture until evenly coated. Dip it in the egg replacer mixture, then roll it in the panko until evenly coated. Set it on a dry plate. Continue with the remaining chunks of cheese, making sure they don't touch when you set them on the plate.

4. **Check the oil temperature.**

When the oil reaches about 375 degrees F, it's ready. If you don't have a kitchen thermometer, test the oil temperature by adding a small piece of cheese to it. If it sinks but rises quickly and steadily to the top, the oil is hot enough. If it sinks to the bottom and lingers there for a moment, the oil isn't yet hot enough.

Per serving: calories: 540, protein: 11 g, fat: 36 g, saturated fat: 4 g, carbohydrate: 43 g, sodium: 222 mg, calcium: 26 mg

5. Fry the cheese.

Once the oil is ready, start adding the cheese, but don't overcrowd the pot; the cheese should cover no more than half the surface. Cook, carefully turning once, until evenly golden brown, about 3 minutes. Drain briefly on paper towels. Serve immediately, with the warm marinara sauce alongside for dipping.

NOTE: Using low-salt or salt-free marinara sauce will decrease the sodium content of this recipe.

In Italy, cooks would be outraged if you didn't eat your pasta or risotto immediately. However, they are also quite inventive when it comes to using leftover risotto that no longer has the perfect texture: they form it into little balls, stuff them with a bit of cheese, and fry until crisp and golden. Presto! The result is *arancini*, aka risotto fritters. While you can make the risotto from scratch, as in this recipe, you can also use leftover risotto. The only requirement is that it be made at least six hours in advance of assembling and frying the *arancini*.

RISOTTO FRITTERS with roasted red bell pepper sauce

MAKES 6 TO 12 SERVINGS

RISOTTO

1 tablespoon extra-virgin olive oil

1 onion, finely chopped

3 cloves garlic, minced

¾ cup Arborio rice

3 cups vegan chicken broth or vegetable broth

1 cup roasted tomatoes or drained and chopped sun-dried tomatoes (see note, page 11)

½ cup slivered fresh basil leaves, lightly packed

Salt

Ground pepper

SAUCE

2 roasted red bell peppers (see sidebar), skinned, seeded, and coarsely chopped

3 to 4 tablespoons extra-virgin olive oil

2 to 3 cloves garlic, coarsely chopped

Salt

1. Make the risotto.

Heat the oil in a medium saucepan over medium heat. Add the onion and garlic, cover, and cook, stirring occasionally, until tender, about 7 minutes. Stir in the rice and cook uncovered, stirring occasionally with a wooden spoon, for 3 to 4 minutes. Pour in ½ cup of the broth and cook, stirring frequently, until the broth is mostly absorbed, about 5 minutes. Continue to add the broth, ½ cup at a time, and cook, stirring frequently, until the broth is mostly absorbed. After adding 2 cups of the broth, stir in the roasted tomatoes. Continue to add the broth, ½ cup at a time, stirring frequently, until all of the broth has been added; the risotto should be thick and creamy and the rice should be tender but firm. (The process from start to finish should take about 30 minutes.) Remove from the heat and stir in the basil. Season with salt and pepper to taste. Pour the risotto into a shallow pan and let cool to room temperature. Cover and refrigerate for at least 6 hours.

2. Make the sauce.

Put the peppers, 3 tablespoons of the oil, and 2 cloves of the garlic in a blender. Process until smooth. Season with salt to taste. Taste and add more oil or garlic if desired.

3. Heat the oil.

Pour oil into a wok or wide pot to a depth of about 2 inches. Put the wok over medium heat.

4. Form the risotto into balls and stuff with cheese.

Using a tablespoon or melon baller, form the chilled risotto into small balls. Poke a hole in each ball with a finger, put a cube of cheese in the middle, then squeeze to enclose the cheese within the risotto. Roll the balls in the polenta until evenly coated.

Use this recipe, which features sun-dried tomatoes and basil, as a stepping-stone to creating your own versions of risotto. The sauce is highly versatile and can enhance many dishes, adding flavor to polenta and pasta, for example. I like to keep some on hand in a squirt bottle so I can use it decorate appetizers and other dishes. As delicious as the sauce is, you could also forgo making it and instead dip the *arancini* in marinara sauce or pesto.

OIL, CHEESE, AND COATING

Canola or grapeseed oil, for frying (3 to 4 cups, depending on the size of the pot)

1 cup cubed cheese (any of the hard or semihard cheeses from chapter 1, 2, or 3), **cut into ½-inch pieces**

1 cup polenta (coarsely ground cornmeal) **or breadcrumbs**

Per serving (based on 9 servings): calories: 388, protein: 5 g, fat: 27 g, saturated fat: 3 g, carbohydrate: 31 g, sodium: 136 mg, calcium: 24 mg

5. Check the oil temperature.

When the oil reaches about 375 degrees F, it's ready. If you don't have a kitchen thermometer, test the oil temperature by adding a grain of rice to it. If it sinks but rises quickly and steadily to the top, the oil is hot enough. If it sinks to the bottom and lingers there for a moment, the oil isn't yet hot enough.

6. Fry the *arancini*.

Once the oil is ready, start adding the *arancini*, but don't overcrowd the pot. Cook, carefully turning once, until evenly golden brown, 2 to 3 minutes. Drain briefly on paper towels. Serve immediately, with the sauce alongside for dipping.

VARIATION: For a lower-fat but less crispy version, preheat the oven to 400 degrees F. Arrange the *arancini* on a baking sheet lined with parchment paper and bake the for about 20 minutes, until golden brown.

Roasting Peppers

- To roast peppers in an oven, preheat the oven to 450 degrees F. Put the peppers on a rimmed baking sheet and bake for 15 to 20 minutes, until puffy and charred in spots, turning them once or twice during the process for even roasting.

- To use a broiler, put an oven rack about 8 inches below the broiler and preheat the broiler. Put the peppers on a rimmed baking sheet and broil, turning often, until evenly charred on all sides.

- To use a grill or the open flame of a gas burner, put the peppers directly on the grill and cook, turning frequently with tongs, until somewhat charred all over.

Once they are roasted, put the peppers in a paper bag and fold down the top, or put them in a bowl and cover with plastic wrap. This will lightly steam the peppers and make them easier to peel. When they are cool enough to handle, remove the skins. Cut the peppers in half and scrape out the seeds and membranes. If you prefer to leave the peppers whole, as for making chiles rellenos or stuffed peppers, cut a slit and carefully scrape out the seeds and membranes through the slit.

In these croquettes, already wonderful Gruyère is enhanced by the smoky, woodsy flavors of mushrooms and the sweetness of sautéed leeks. Served in bite-sized portions, this makes a fabulous appetizer, or make larger croquettes for a great entrée.

PORCINI, LEEK, AND GRUYÈRE croquettes

MAKES 10 TO 12 SERVINGS AS AN APPE-
TIZER, OR 5 TO 6 SERVINGS AS AN ENTRÉE

CROQUETTE BASE

½ cup dried porcini mushrooms

½ cup dried matsutake mushrooms
or more porcini mushrooms

2 leeks, white parts only, halved
lengthwise and thinly sliced

Salt

2 tablespoons pale dry sherry

2 cups Soft Gruyère (page 13) or coarsely
chopped Hard Gruyère (page 13)

Ground pepper

DIPPING COMPONENTS
AND OIL

1 cup flour

½ cup water

¼ cup Ener-G egg replacer
(see page 134)

2 cups panko

Canola or grapeseed oil, for frying
(3 to 4 cups, depending on the size of
the pot)

1. **Reconstitute the mushrooms.**
Soak the dried mushrooms in about 2 cups of hot water until soft, about 20 minutes. Drain, reserving the liquid. Chop the mushrooms into ½-inch pieces.

2. **Cook the leeks and mushrooms.**
Heat about 3 tablespoons of the mushroom soaking liquid in a medium skillet over medium heat. (Save the rest of the mushroom liquid for another use, such as in a soup or sauce, or as part of the liquid when cooking grains.) Add the leeks, sprinkle with a pinch of salt, and cook, stirring occasionally, until tender, about 5 minutes. Add the mushrooms and sherry and cook, stirring frequently, until most of the liquid has cooked off, about 5 minutes. Remove from the heat and stir in the Gruyère. Season with salt and pepper to taste. Transfer to a container, cover, and refrigerate until firm, at least 2 hours.

3. **Shape into logs.**
Transfer the chilled mixture to a large sheet of plastic wrap and shape into a log with a diameter of 1 to 1½ inches for serving as an appetizer, or 3 inches for serving as an entrée. Wrap tightly in the plastic wrap and freeze for at least 2 hours.

4. **Set up the dipping components.**
To set up a three-dip fry station, put the flour in a small bowl. Put the water and egg replacer in a second small bowl and whisk vigorously until frothy and thick. Put the panko in a third small bowl.

Per serving (based on 12 servings): calories: 326, protein: 5 g, fat: 20 g, saturated fat: 3 g, carbohydrate: 31 g, sodium: 153 mg, calcium: 17 mg

Give yourself a head start and make the base the day before you plan to fry and serve these, or the croquettes can turn into a sticky mess. If you simply must prepare and serve them on a shorter timeline, put the cooked vegetable mixture in the freezer for at least two hours before attempting to shape it into a log. Although the mixture is a bit difficult to work with, the results are worth the trouble. The croquettes are so delicious and creamy that they are excellent on their own, without any sauce.

5. Heat the oil.

Pour oil into a wok or wide pot to a depth of about 2 inches. Put the wok over medium heat.

6. Slice and coat the croquettes.

Remove the log from the freezer and slice it ¼ inch thick for serving as an appetizer, or ½ to ¾ inch thick for serving as an entrée. Working quickly so the slices don't thaw and get messy, dredge each slice in the flour until evenly coated, then dip in the egg replacer, then coat evenly with the panko.

7. Check the oil temperature.

When the oil reaches about 375 degrees F, it's ready. If you don't have a kitchen thermometer, test the oil temperature by adding a small piece of one croquette to it. If it sinks but rises quickly and steadily to the top, the oil is hot enough. If it sinks to the bottom and lingers there for a moment, the oil isn't yet hot enough.

8. Fry the croquettes.

Once the oil is ready, carefully lower the croquettes into the oil and cook, carefully turning once, until golden brown, about 3 minutes. Drain briefly on paper towels. Serve immediately.

Some things never go out of food fashion, and Brie en croûte is one of them. After all, who can resist this mouthwatering French dish of a round of Brie encased in buttery puff pastry and baked to perfection? Needless to say, the usual version, made with dairy-based Brie, is so rich that it should only be consumed in small amounts as an appetizer. Because this vegan version is lighter, it is also suitable for a first course or even an entrée.

While you can make this plain, I recommend including a filling for even more flavor and pizzazz. The combination of dried fruit and nuts in the main recipe is a classic, creating a truly festive appetizer fit for a holiday buffet. However, there are many other delectable possibilities, so I also provide three alternatives in the variations. If you use the mushroom filling or caramelized onion filling, you can turn this appetizer into

BRIE EN CROÛTE with dried fruit and nuts

MAKES ABOUT 20 SERVINGS AS AN APPETIZER, OR ABOUT 6 SERVINGS AS A FIRST COURSE OR ENTRÉE

DRIED FRUIT AND NUT FILLING

2 tablespoons brandy (optional)

1 cup dried cranberries or cherries

1 tablespoon canola oil

⅔ cup walnuts or pecans, chopped

Salt

⅓ cup apricot, cherry, or peach preserves (optional)

PASTRY AND CHEESE

1 sheet (about 8 inches square) packaged vegan puff pastry, thawed according to the package directions

One 6-inch round Air-Dried Brie (page 39) or Air-Dried Camembert (page 38)

Soy milk, for brushing

1. **Prepare the filling.**

If using the optional brandy, put the cranberries in a small bowl, sprinkle the brandy over them, and toss to coat. Let rest for about 30 minutes. Heat the oil in a small skillet over medium heat. Add the walnuts and cook, stirring frequently, until lightly browned, 3 to 4 minutes. Season with salt to taste. Gently stir the walnuts into the cranberries.

2. **Preheat the oven.**

Preheat the oven to 375 degrees F.

3. **Encase the cheese and filling.**

Lightly flour a work surface. Gently transfer the pastry dough to the work surface and roll out to a square about 10 inches across. Place the round of cheese in the center of the dough. Spread the optional jam evenly over the top of the cheese. Scatter the cranberries and walnuts evenly over the jam. Brush a little soy milk on each corner of the dough, then gather all four corners and gently pull the dough up and over the cheese and filling. Twist the corners at the top to form a little bundle. Lightly brush soy milk over the top. Transfer to a baking sheet.

4. **Bake.**

Bake for 25 to 30 minutes, until puffed and golden brown. Cut into thin wedges and serve warm.

Per serving (based on 20 servings with fruit and nut filling): calories: 152, protein: 3 g, fat: 12 g, saturated fat: 2 g, carbohydrate: 9 g, sodium: 198 mg, calcium: 21 mg

a spectacular lunch or light supper by serving it with a salad. Or, for a special dessert on a warm summer evening, try the stone fruit filling; in that variation, this recipe could be considered a very elegant rendition of a wedge of cheese with a slice of fruit pie, and fit to be accompanied by a glass of champagne.

Note that the instructions in this recipe call for spreading the filling atop the cheese; however, you can also slice the cheese in half horizontally and sandwich the filling within the cheese. The puff pastry that's readily available in the freezer section at grocery stores, made by various major food manufacturers, is generally vegan. Just read the ingredients list on the label to be sure. Alternatively, you can also use a homemade flaky pie crust. Admittedly, puff pastry definitely isn't one of the most healthful foods on the planet, but this Brie en croûte might serve as adequate justification to eat it once in a while.

MUSHROOM FILLING: Dice 12 ounces of mushrooms, preferably a variety, such as chanterelles, cremini, morels, and porcini. Heat 1 tablespoon of extra-virgin olive oil in a large skillet over medium-high heat. Add the mushrooms, a couple of pinches of salt, and 2 to 3 cloves of garlic, minced. Cook, stirring frequently, until the mushrooms are tender and browned, about 7 minutes. (Be sure to keep the heat high so the mushrooms don't end up watery, rather than brown; if they stick a bit, that's okay.) Stir in 1 teaspoon of chopped fresh thyme, then sprinkle 2 tablespoons of dry sherry, Marsala, or Madeira over the mushrooms and stir to loosen any bits that have stuck to the pan. Season with salt and pepper to taste.

CARAMELIZED ONION FILLING: Caramelized onions offer a wonderful sweetness that offsets the slight sharpness of the cheese, especially the Camembert. To prepare a caramelized onion filling, thinly slice 2 onions. Heat 1 tablespoon of canola oil in a heavy medium skillet over medium-high heat. Add the onions and a couple of pinches of salt and cook over medium-high heat, stirring frequently, until wilted, about 5 minutes. Decrease the heat to medium and cook, stirring frequently, until deep golden brown, about 15 minutes. (If the onions stick a bit, that's okay.) Sprinkle about 3 tablespoons of dry red wine over the onions and stir to loosen any bits that have stuck to the pan. (You can use water instead of wine, but I recommend the wine for additional flavor complexity.) Cook, stirring frequently, for another minute to allow the onions to absorb the wine. Stir in 1 teaspoon of chopped fresh thyme if you like, then season with salt and pepper to taste.

STONE FRUIT FILLING: You'll need 6 apricots or 2 peaches for this filling. Be sure to use ripe but firm fruit so it will be flavorful but not too soft after baking. Slice the fruit a generous ¼ inch thick. I don't peel the fruit, but it's fine to do so if you prefer. Sprinkle 2 tablespoons of sugar and 1 tablespoon of all-purpose flour over the fruit and toss gently until the fruit is evenly coated. Before topping the cheese with the fruit, spread about ¼ cup of apricot or peach preserves evenly over the cheese, then pile the fruit on top in an even layer.

This terrific appetizer also works well as an entrée; just serve two halves per person. It's also great party fare because you can cook the artichokes up to two days ahead of time. Then it takes only five minutes to put the filling together, leaving you more time for final preparations for the party.

ARTICHOKES stuffed with almonds and cheese

MAKES 6 SERVINGS

3 large artichokes

½ teaspoon salt

4 ounces Meltable Cheddar (page 43), cut into ½-inch chunks

¾ cup raw almonds

½ cup fresh basil leaves, lightly packed

2 cloves garlic, coarsely chopped

1. **Cook the artichokes.**

Trim the artichokes, paring away any tough portions of the stem and cutting off the top ½ to 1 inch of each artichoke. Remove any remaining spiky tips with kitchen scissors. Cut the artichokes in half lengthwise. Put them in a large pot and add water to cover, along with the salt. Cover and bring to a boil over medium-high heat. Decrease the heat to medium-low and simmer until the artichokes are tender, about 30 minutes. Drain and let sit until cool enough to handle. (If not using right away, store in a covered container in the refrigerator for up to 2 days.)

2. **Preheat the oven.**

Preheat the oven to 375 degrees F.

3. **Make the filling.**

Put the cheese, almonds, basil, and garlic in a food processor. Process briefly, until the almonds are coarsely chopped and all the ingredients are thoroughly combined. Some of the almonds should still be slightly chunky.

4. **Stuff and bake the artichokes.**

Using a spoon, scoop out and discard the hairy choke from each artichoke half. Stuff the hollows with the filling, dividing it evenly among them. Put the artichokes in a 13 x 9-inch baking pan and bake for about 45 minutes, until the filling is browned. To eat, scoop up the filling with the leaves.

Per serving: calories: 201, protein: 9 g, fat: 13 g, saturated fat: 1 g, carbohydrate: 10 g, sodium: 408 mg, calcium: 107 mg

8

Entrées and Accompaniments

Get ready for big, hearty, cheesy flavors in a variety of traditional, classic dishes. My love for all things Italian expresses itself in this chapter, and you'll also find homey comfort foods like macaroni and cheese that will take you back to your childhood. These recipes reveal that the cheeses in this book can be used just like their dairy counterparts, whether in hearty Eggplant Parmesan (page 92) or Chiles Rellenos with Ranchero Sauce (page 100), producing dishes that are rich and satisfying.

Mac and cheese is hard to beat as a comfort food. It holds a dear place in the heart of my husband, who grew up loving his dad's version of this classic. With the help of my Sharp Cheddar, I was finally able to create a vegan version that my husband finds equally satisfying. This dish is definitely a good reason to always have some homemade vegan Sharp Cheddar around!

classic baked MACARONI AND CHEESE

MAKES ABOUT 6 SERVINGS

1 tablespoon salt (optional)

1 pound macaroni, small pasta shells, or penne

1 pound Sharp Cheddar (page 14), grated

2 cups plain, unsweetened soy milk

Salt (optional)

Ground pepper (optional)

1. Cook the macaroni.

Bring a large pot of water to a boil over high heat. Add the optional salt, then stir in the macaroni. Return to a boil. Decrease the heat to medium-low and cook, stirring occasionally, until tender but firm, about 8 minutes. Drain in a colander and rinse under cold water.

2. Assemble and bake.

Preheat the oven to 350 degrees F. Spread half of the pasta in a 13 x 9-inch baking pan. Scatter half of the cheese evenly over the pasta. Top with the remaining pasta, then scatter the remaining cheese over the top. Pour in the soy milk. Sprinkle salt and pepper over the top if desired. Cover and bake for about 30 minutes. Uncover and bake for 10 to 15 more minutes, until the top is browned and crispy. Serve immediately.

Per serving: calories: 442, protein: 19 g, fat: 23 g, saturated fat: 4 g, carbohydrate: 42 g, sodium: 569 mg, calcium: 56 mg

Creamy, rich, and succulent, this pasta dish is the perfect supper, yet it's ever so easy to put together. The beauty of this dish is that you don't even need to culture the Soft Gruyère. On the other hand, if you already have some vegan Gruyère in the fridge and want to use it in something delectable, it will also work well here.

FETTUCCINE ALFREDO with gruyère and mushrooms

MAKES 6 TO 8 SERVINGS

1 tablespoon salt (optional), **plus more as desired**

1 pound fettuccine or linguine

1 tablespoon extra-virgin olive oil

8 ounces morel, cremini, or button mushrooms, sliced

2 tablespoons dry sherry

1 pound Soft Gruyère (page 13), **made through step 1** (no need to let it culture), **or Hard Gruyère** (page 13)

1. Cook the pasta.

Bring a large pot of water to a boil over high heat. Add the optional salt, then stir in the fettuccine. Return to a boil. Decrease the heat to medium-low and cook, stirring occasionally, until tender but firm, about 8 minutes. Ladle out and reserve 2 cups of the pasta water, then drain the fettuccine in a colander and rinse under cold water. Transfer to a large bowl.

2. Sauté the mushrooms while the pasta is cooking.

Heat the oil in a medium skillet over medium-high heat. Add the mushrooms and cook, stirring frequently for 1 minute. Sprinkle a couple of pinches of salt over the mushrooms and cook, stirring occasionally, until browned, about 7 minutes. Sprinkle the sherry over the mushrooms and stir to loosen any bits that have stuck to the pan.

3. Make the sauce.

Combine the cheese and 1 cup of the reserved pasta water in a heavy medium saucepan over medium heat. Cook, stirring constantly with a wooden spoon, until the cheese is melted and the sauce is thick, about 5 minutes. Add more of the pasta water as needed to achieve the desired consistency.

4. Assemble the dish.

Add the sauce to the pasta and toss until evenly coated. Portion among plates or shallow bowls and top each serving with a spoonful of the mushrooms. Serve immediately.

Per serving (based on 7 servings): calories: 407, protein: 11 g, fat: 26 g, saturated fat: 9 g, carbohydrate: 29 g, sodium: 436 mg, calcium: 26 mg

Here I offer a lighter version of this classic dish. Instead of coating the eggplant in flour or breadcrumbs and frying it in lots of oil, it is roasted, substantially reducing the amount of oil required and producing a lighter, more fresh-tasting dish. This also eliminates the need to salt the eggplant in advance, as called for in many recipes. The result is a dish that's faster and easier to assemble. It's even tastier reheated the next day, once the flavors have had a chance to meld.

EGGPLANT parmesan

MAKES 8 SERVINGS

2 pounds eggplant, preferably Japanese or Italian, sliced a generous ¼ inch thick

Extra-virgin olive oil

Salt

Ground pepper

4½ cups marinara sauce (see note)

¼ cup fresh basil leaves, lightly packed

12 ounces Meltable Mozzarella (page 44) or Meltable Muenster (page 41), sliced ¼ inch thick or grated

1. **Roast the eggplant.**
Preheat the oven to 450 degrees F. Line two or three baking sheets with parchment paper. Arrange the eggplant in a single layer on the baking sheets. Lightly brush the slices with the oil, then turn and lightly brush the other side. Sprinkle with salt and pepper. Bake for 15 to 20 minutes, until fork-tender.

2. **Assemble the dish.**
Decrease the oven temperature to 400 degrees F. Spread 1 cup of the marinara sauce evenly in a 13 x 9-inch baking pan. Layer half of the eggplant slices over the marinara sauce. Spread 1½ cups of the marinara sauce over the eggplant, then scatter half of the basil over the sauce. Layer half of the cheese evenly over the sauce and top with the remaining eggplant. Spread the remaining 2 cups of sauce over the eggplant, then scatter the remaining basil over the sauce. Layer the remaining cheese evenly over the top.

3. **Bake.**
Bake uncovered for about 30 minutes, until the sauce is bubbly and the cheese on top is browned. Serve immediately.

NOTE: You can decrease the amount of baking time to about 20 minutes if you heat the marinara sauce before assembling the dish.

Per serving: calories: 194, protein: 4 g, fat: 11 g, saturated fat: 1 g, carbohydrate: 17 g, sodium: 862 mg, calcium: 83 mg
Note: Using low-salt or salt-free marinara sauce will decrease the sodium content of this recipe.

Pizza Margherita, *page 94*

Stuffed Shells, *facing page*

This quick and easy dish is a favorite in my cooking classes. Pasta stuffed with light and fluffy Almond Ricotta and liberally doused with marinara sauce is a truly satisfying entrée. Although this recipe calls for large pasta shells, feel free to substitute other shapes, such as manicotti or cannelloni.

stuffed SHELLS

See photo on facing page.

See photo on facing page.

MAKES 6 TO 8 SERVINGS

1 pound large pasta shells

Salt

4 cups Almond Ricotta (page 47)

¼ cup slivered fresh basil leaves, lightly packed

2 tablespoons nutritional yeast flakes

1 to 2 tablespoons freshly squeezed lemon juice

2 cloves garlic, minced

Ground pepper

8 cups marinara sauce

8 ounces Meltable Mozzarella (page 44), **grated** (optional)

1. **Cook the pasta shells.**

Bring a large pot of water to a boil over high heat. Add 1 tablespoon of salt if desired, then add the pasta shells. Return to a boil. Decrease the heat to medium-low and cook, stirring occasionally, until tender but firm, about 12 minutes. Drain in a colander and rinse under cold water.

2. **Make the filling.**

Put the ricotta, basil, nutritional yeast, lemon juice, and garlic in a large bowl and mix well. Season with salt and pepper to taste.

3. **Fill the shells and bake.**

Preheat the oven to 375 degrees F. Stuff the cooked pasta shells with the filling, dividing it evenly among them. Spread 2 cups of the marinara sauce evenly in a 13 x 9-inch baking pan, then arrange the stuffed shells atop the marinara sauce. Pour the remaining 6 cups of marinara sauce evenly over the pasta shells. Sprinkle the optional mozzarella evenly over the top. Cover and bake for 25 to 30 minutes, until hot and bubbling. Serve immediately.

Per serving (based on 7 servings): calories: 569, protein: 18 g, fat: 36 g, saturated fat: 3 g, carbohydrate: 42 g, sodium: 1,314 mg, calcium: 224 mg

Note: Using low-salt or salt-free marinara sauce will decrease the sodium content of this recipe.

Gnocchi are light and wonderful Italian dumplings often made from potatoes. In this recipe the dough is flavored with Hard Gruyère or Sharp Cheddar. The result is rich and full-flavored gnocchi that are well-complemented by any number of sauces. If you make the gnocchi with Sharp Cheddar, try topping them with marinara sauce.

cheese GNOCCHI

MAKES 6 SERVINGS

2 pounds Yukon gold or other waxy potatoes, scrubbed

10 ounces Hard Gruyère (page 13) or Sharp Cheddar (page 14), diced or grated (see note)

1 cup all-purpose flour

2 tablespoons nutritional yeast flakes

1 teaspoon salt, plus more for boiling if desired

1. **Cook the potatoes.**

Put the potatoes in a large pot and add water to cover by a few inches. Bring to a boil over high heat. Decrease the heat to medium-low, cover, and cook until fork-tender, 20 to 30 minutes. Drain well and let sit just until cool enough to handle. (The potatoes should still be fairly hot when mashed and mixed with the remaining ingredients.) Cut the potatoes in half and peel them by hand; the skins should slip off easily.

2. **Mash or rice the potatoes.**

Put the potatoes in a large bowl and mash with a potato masher until smooth and lump-free; alternatively, if you have a ricer, use that, as it will yield the lightest, fluffiest, and smoothest texture. (Don't use a food processor, or the potatoes may get gluey.)

3. **Make the dough.**

While the potatoes are still hot, add the cheese and mix well. Add the flour, nutritional yeast, and salt and mix well with your hands. Turn out onto an unfloured work surface and knead until soft and pliable, about 2 minutes.

4. **Shape the gnocchi.**

Form the dough into a ball, then cut it into four equal portions. Roll each portion into a log about 1 foot long and ¾ inch in diameter. Cut each log into pieces a scant ½ inch thick. Cutting will press the dough down, resulting in oval or semicircular pieces. If you aren't

Per serving: calories: 443, protein: 13 g, fat: 20 g, saturated fat: 7 g, carbohydrate: 52 g, sodium: 708 mg, calcium: 20 mg

For gnocchi made with Soft Gruyère, try Rich and Creamy Alfredo Sauce (page 62) or vegan pesto, or simply drizzle with olive oil and season with minced garlic and minced fresh sage. Gnocchi are actually easy and quite fast to make, and a fun alternative to pasta. Be aware that they don't freeze well. However, you can make them up to three hours before boiling and serving.

going to cook the gnocchi immediately, put the pieces on a lightly floured board in a single layer and cover with a clean kitchen towel for up to 3 hours, until you're ready to cook them.

5. Cook the gnocchi.

Bring a large pot of water to a boil over high heat. Add salt if desired, then stir in half of the gnocchi. They will sink to the bottom of the pot; then, in 2 to 4 minutes they will start to float. Using a slotted spoon, remove and drain the gnocchi as they rise to the surface. Repeat with the remaining gnocchi. Serve immediately.

NOTE: You can also use Soft Gruyère (page 13) or Crock-Style Cheddar (page 15) in this recipe. Because both are soft, just stir them in as is, rather than trying to dice or grate them.

Even if you're not in Rome, do as the Romans and try making gnocchi from semolina instead of potatoes. Semolina is durum wheat, a high-protein, hard, winter wheat, that's ground to a texture similar to uncooked farina. In fact, this creamy and savory dish is actually made by cooking the semolina like farina or polenta. Although many people think of gnocchi solely as small dumplings, the dough can also be spread in a pan,

GNOCCHI à la romana

MAKES 6 SERVINGS

2 cups vegan chicken broth

1 cup plain, unsweetened soy milk

¼ cup vegan buttery spread or extra-virgin olive oil (optional)

1 cup semolina

¾ cup Cashew Cream (page 55) or additional soy milk

½ teaspoon salt

8 ounces meltable cheese from chapter 3 (any variety), grated

1. **Cook the semolina.**

Put the broth, soy milk, and optional buttery spread in a heavy medium saucepan and bring to a boil over medium-high heat. Decrease the heat to medium-low and add the semolina in a thin, steady stream, whisking constantly to prevent lumping. Add the Cashew Cream and salt, still whisking continuously. As the mixture thickens, switch to a wooden spoon and cook, stirring almost constantly, until very thick, 15 to 20 minutes.

2. **Pour into a pan to set.**

Oil a 13 x 9-inch baking pan or line it with parchment paper. Pour in the semolina mixture while still hot. Spread it in an even layer and smooth the top. Let cool completely at room temperature, then cover and let rest for about 7 hours, until firm. If your kitchen is very warm (over 75 degrees F), put the dough in the refrigerator to firm up; otherwise you can just leave it on the counter.

3. **Shape and bake the gnocchi.**

Preheat the oven to 350 degrees F. Cut the gnocchi into 12 pieces with a knife, or use a 3-inch round cookie cutter to cut it into 12 circles. Arrange the pieces in the same baking pan, slightly overlapping. (If you lined the pan with parchment, discard it before arranging the pieces in the pan.) Sprinkle the cheese evenly over the top. Bake for about 20 minutes, until the cheese is bubbly and melted. Serve immediately.

Per serving: calories: 262, protein: 10 g, fat: 10 g, saturated fat: 1 g, carbohydrate: 32 g, sodium: 584 mg, calcium: 48 mg

cooled, and then cut into pieces that are fried or, as in this recipe, baked—with vegan cheese on top, of course! If you like, you can flavor the base with mushrooms, leeks, or sun-dried tomatoes, as described in the variations. Be aware that the dough must sit for at least seven hours to firm up, so you'll need to plan ahead.

GNOCCHI À LA ROMANA WITH TRUFFLED MUSHROOMS: Thinly slice 8 ounces of mushrooms. Heat 2 teaspoons of extra-virgin olive oil in a medium skillet over medium-high heat. Add the mushrooms and a couple of pinches of salt and cook, stirring frequently, until tender and browned, about 7 minutes. At the end of step 1, before pouring the semolina mixture into the baking pan, stir in the mushrooms and 1 teaspoon of truffle oil.

GNOCCHI À LA ROMANA WITH LEEKS: Thinly slice the white portion of 1 to 2 leeks. Heat 2 teaspoons of extra-virgin olive oil in a medium skillet over medium-high heat. Add the leeks and a couple of pinches of salt and cook, stirring frequently, until tender, about 5 minutes. Season with pepper to taste. At the end of step 1, before pouring the semolina mixture into the baking pan, stir in the leeks.

GNOCCHI À LA ROMANA WITH SUN-DRIED TOMATOES AND BASIL: Drain and chop ½ cup of oil-packed sun-dried tomatoes; alternatively, soak ½ cup of dry sun-dried tomatoes in hot water for 1 hour, then drain and chop. Sliver ½ cup of lightly packed fresh basil leaves and mince 2 to 3 cloves of garlic. At the end of step 1, before pouring the semolina mixture into the baking pan, stir in the sun-dried tomatoes, basil, and garlic.

MINI GNOCCHI: To serve this dish as an appetizer, use the smallest cookie cutter you can find and cut the gnocchi into small pieces. Instead of baking them, sauté them in olive oil on both sides until golden brown. Serve topped with vegan pesto, caponata, or other savory toppings. This makes about 12 appetizer servings.

Homemade ravioli is within the realm of possibility for most home cooks and doesn't require expensive equipment. In fact, you don't even need to make your own pasta. Purchase sheets of fresh vegan pasta, if you can find it, or make the ravioli with vegan wonton or pot sticker wrappers. If you use one of those options, this dish will require only about twenty minutes of hands-on time. Best of all, the combination of the simple filling and sauce is superb.

BUTTERNUT SQUASH AND GRUYÈRE RAVIOLI
with shallot and thyme béchamel

MAKES 4 TO 5 SERVINGS

RAVIOLI

1 pound butternut squash, peeled and cubed

1 tablespoon extra-virgin olive oil

Salt

Ground pepper

8 ounces fresh vegan pasta sheets (see notes)

6 ounces Hard Gruyère (page 13), grated or diced, or Soft Gruyère (page 13)

SAUCE

2 teaspoons extra-virgin olive oil

⅔ cup finely chopped shallots

Salt

Ground pepper

2 cups Cashew Cream (page 55)

1 teaspoon minced fresh thyme, or ½ teaspoon dried

1. **Bake the squash.**

Preheat the oven to 425 degrees F. Put the squash on a rimmed baking sheet or in a baking pan large enough to accommodate all of it in a single layer. Drizzle the oil evenly over the squash, then season with salt and pepper. Toss until evenly coated, then spread in a single layer. Bake for about 20 minutes, until browned on the bottom and tender.

2. **Fill the ravioli.**

Cut the pasta sheets into 4-inch squares; you should have 8 to 10 squares. Using your finger, dab water all along the edges of one square. Put about 2 tablespoons of the squash on one side of the square and top with 1½ tablespoons of the cheese. Fold the pasta square over the filling to encase it completely, then press the edges together. Crimp the edges all the way around with the tines of a fork to ensure a secure seal. Repeat with the remaining pasta, squash, and cheese.

3. **Make the sauce.**

Heat the oil in a heavy medium saucepan over medium heat. Add the shallots, cover, and cook, stirring occasionally, until translucent and tender, about 5 minutes. Season with salt and pepper. Add the Cashew Cream and cook uncovered, stirring frequently, until the mixture thickens and begins to bubble, about 5 minutes. Add the thyme and cook, stirring frequently, for 1 minute. Taste and add more salt and pepper if desired.

Per serving: calories: 545, protein: 15 g, fat: 29 g, saturated fat: 8 g, carbohydrate: 56 g, sodium: 522 mg, calcium: 67 mg

The sweet, rich, buttery flavor of the slightly caramelized squash pairs beautifully with the delicious vegan Gruyère, and smothering the ravioli in a creamy, savory sauce infused with shallots and thyme takes this dish over the top. Both the ravioli and the sauce can be made up to a day in advance if you like (see notes).

4. Cock the ravioli.

Bring a large pot of water to a boil over high heat. Add 1 tablespoon of salt if desired, then add the ravioli. Return to a boil. Decrease the heat to medium-low and cook, stirring gently from time to time, until the pasta is tender, 3 to 5 minutes. Drain in a colander. Portion the ravioli among plates or shallow bowls and pour the sauce on top, dividing it evenly. Serve immediately.

NOTES: One of the best parts about making ravioli is customizing them to suit your tastes and making use of ingredients that are in season or readily available.

- When working with fresh pasta sheets, the size and shape of the ravioli can be varied as you desire. The method here makes 8 to 10 large ravioli. If you choose to make them a different size, adjust the amount of filling accordingly.

- To make the ravioli using vegan wonton or pot sticker wrappers in place of the pasta sheets, you'll need about 24 wrappers. Dab a bit of water all along the edges of one wrapper. Put a heaping 1 tablespoon of the squash on one side of the wrapper and top with about 1 tablespoon of the cheese. Fold the wrapper over the filling to encase it completely and press the edges together. Crimp the edges all the way around with the tines of a fork to ensure a secure seal. Repeat with the remaining wrappers, squash, and cheese.

- You can make both the ravioli and the sauce up to a day in advance. If you aren't going to cook the ravioli right away, dust a plate with flour and arrange the ravioli on the plate, leaving a little room between them. Cover with a clean kitchen towel and let sit at room temperature for up to 3 hours or store in the refrigerator for up to 1 day. After making the sauce, let it cool completely at room temperature, then store in a covered container in the refrigerator for up to 1 day. Gently reheat the sauce before assembling the dish.

Pizza in Italy is an entirely different creature from what you find in the United States. There, the best pizzas have but a smear of marinara sauce and only a hint of cheese, whereas American versions tend to be piled high with toppings and as much gooey, oily, stretchy cheese as the crust can hold. This thin-crust pizza is more akin to those made in Naples (often considered the birthplace of pizza) than those made in New York. Topped with vegan cheese that bubbles, melts, and browns, it looks so much like dairy pizza that even skeptical teenagers enjoy it.

One of the tricks to a decent homemade pizza is using a pizza stone. These are inexpensive and can be purchased at most cookware stores or online. Heating the stone at a high temperature for about

pizza MARGHERITA

See photo facing page 86.

MAKES TWO 14-INCH PIZZAS (3 SERVINGS EACH), OR SIX INDIVIDUAL 6-INCH PIZZAS

DOUGH

4 cups bread flour, plus more for dusting and shaping

1½ teaspoons salt

1 teaspoon active dry yeast

1½ cups cold water

TOPPINGS

2 cups marinara sauce

14 ounces Meltable Mozzarella (page 44), **sliced**

½ cup plus 1 tablespoon slivered fresh basil leaves, lightly packed

Per serving (based on 8 servings): calories: 396, protein: 10 g, fat: 12 g, saturated fat: 1 g, carbohydrate: 60 g, sodium: 976 mg, calcium: 73 mg

Note: Using low-salt or salt-free marinara sauce will decrease the sodium content of this recipe.

1. **Make the dough.**

Put the flour, salt, and yeast in a large bowl or the bowl of an electric mixer and stir with a large spoon until well mixed. Add the cold water and stir until well combined. To knead by hand, turn the dough out onto a floured work surface and knead until smooth and pliable, about 7 minutes, occasionally dusting with a bit of flour to prevent sticking; if using a stand mixer, mix with the dough hook until smooth and pliable, about 6 minutes. Immediately wrap the dough in plastic wrap or a clean plastic bag and refrigerate for at least 2 hours and up to 2 days, without letting it rise before refrigerating; this delays the rising until the pizza is in the oven, creating the optimum texture.

2. **Heat the pizza stone.**

Preheat the oven to 450 degrees F. Then heat a pizza stone on the lowest rack for 45 minutes. (If you don't have a pizza stone, see notes.)

3. **Prepare a pizza assembly station.**

About 20 minutes before serving the first pizza, assemble the toppings. Pull the dough out of the refrigerator and cut it into two equal pieces for 14-inch pizzas, or six equal pieces for individual pizzas. Shape the pieces into balls. Generously flour a work surface, lightly flour a pizza peel (see notes), and dust your hands and wrists with flour.

4. **Shape the dough.**

To ensure optimum results, it's best to bake one pizza at a time so the oven stays as hot as possible. You can shape and top one pizza, then continue with shaping and topping as the first pizza bakes. Put one of the dough balls on the floured work surface and press to flatten it a bit, then turn it so both sides are well coated with flour. Form a fist with one hand, pick up the dough with your other hand, and put the dough over your fist. Gently pull and rotate the dough, stretching

forty-five minutes before you're ready to bake the pizza will ensure a crisp bottom and quick baking. If you don't have a pizza stone, you can still make delicious pizza (see notes), but the crust won't be as crisp on the bottom. Whatever baking method you choose, just don't go hog wild with the toppings. Plus, you don't need a lot of toppings when all of the components are delicious. In general, use less than a cup of toppings (in addition to the sauce and vegan cheese) per fourteen-inch pizza. As long as you follow that guideline, you can experiment and use whatever toppings you like: olives, artichoke hearts, caramelized onions . . . you name it! One final pointer: The dough for the crust needs to rest for two hours, so you'll need to plan ahead.

and enlarging it until you've formed a thin, even round about 14 inches in diameter, or about 6 inches in diameter for an individual pizza. Don't worry if there are a few small tears. Put the dough on the floured peel and pinch together any tears to seal the dough back together.

5. Top the pizza.

Spread the marinara sauce over the surface to within ½ inch of the edge, using 1 cup of sauce for a 14-inch pizza, or ⅓ cup for a 6-inch pizza. Top with the mozzarella, using 7 ounces of cheese for a 14-inch pizza, or 2⅓ ounces for a 6-inch pizza. Scatter the basil equally over the pizzas.

6. Bake the pizza.

Give the peel a quick shake to ensure that the pizza will slide off. If it appears to be sticking, work a bit more flour underneath the sticky spot, then give it another quick shake to make sure it will slide off. Transfer the pizza to the oven, sliding it off the peel and onto the stone. Bake for about 8 minutes, until the crust is lightly browned on the edges and the cheese is melted, bubbly, and lightly browned. (The baking time is the same for 14-inch and 6-inch pizzas.) Let cool for a minute or two before serving.

MUSHROOM PIZZA: Scatter about ¾ cup of thinly sliced mushrooms over the cheese atop one 14-inch pizza before baking. Experiment with a variety of mushrooms. Enticing choices include oyster mushrooms, shiitakes, and chanterelles.

PIZZA WITH CHARD AND GARLIC: Toss 1 cup of coarsely chopped Swiss chard with 1 teaspoon of extra-virgin olive oil, 1 clove of garlic, minced, and a sprinkling of salt. Scatter the mixture over the cheese atop one 14-inch pizza before baking.

NOTES: Although a pizza stone and a peel are wonderful tools for making pizza, you can definitely get by without any special equipment.

- If you don't have a pizza stone, you can simulate the thermal mass of a pizza stone with a large, heavy cast-iron skillet. Put an oven rack in the middle of the oven, and put the skillet on the rack, inverting it. Preheat the oven to 500 degrees F for at least 30 minutes. Put shaped 14-inch crusts on round pizza pans or a very large baking sheet, and put smaller 6-inch crusts on sheet pans. Apply the toppings to the pizzas on the pans, then put the pans on top of the inverted skillet for baking, one pan at a time.

- If you have a pizza stone, you probably have a peel as well. If you don't, no problem. Once the dough is shaped, put it on a lightly floured cutting board and add the toppings. You can use the cutting board like a peel to transfer the topped pizza to the oven and slide it onto the stone.

A calzone is basically a pizza folded over, so any topping that goes on a pizza can go in a calzone. That makes this a very flexible recipe; you can use any cooked vegetable, including bell peppers, broccoli, chard, mushrooms, onions, or spinach. Instead of ricotta, you could use Meltable Mozzarella (page 44) or any cheese from chapter 3. This recipe features a cornmeal and spelt dough as a creative touch and for enhanced nutrition; however you can use any pizza dough you like (including the one on page 94).

chard and ricotta CALZONES

MAKES 8 SERVINGS

DOUGH

1 cup cold water

1 tablespoon active dry yeast

1 teaspoon maple syrup, agave nectar, or sugar

2 tablespoons extra-virgin olive oil

½ teaspoon salt

1½ cups cornmeal

1½ cups whole spelt flour, plus more for dusting and shaping

2 tablespoons vital wheat gluten (see note)

Per serving: calories: 328, protein: 13 g, fat: 13 g, saturated fat: 1 g, carbohydrate: 38 g, sodium: 370 mg, calcium: 76 mg

Note: Using low-salt or salt-free marinara sauce will decrease the sodium content of this recipe.

1. **Make the dough.**

Put the water, yeast, and maple syrup in a large bowl or the bowl of an electric mixer and mix lightly. Let rest for about 5 minutes. Add the oil and salt and mix until thoroughly blended. Add the cornmeal, spelt flour, and gluten and stir until well combined. To knead by hand, turn the dough out onto a floured work surface and knead until smooth and pliable, about 7 minutes, occasionally dusting with a bit of flour to prevent sticking; if using a stand mixer, mix with the dough hook until smooth and pliable, about 6 minutes. The dough will be fairly stiff. Transfer to a clean, lightly oiled bowl, cover with a clean kitchen towel, and let rise in a warm place until almost doubled in size, about 1 hour.

2. **Cook the chard for the filling.**

Heat the water in a large skillet over medium-high heat until it sizzles. Add 4 cloves of the garlic and the chard and sprinkle with a couple of pinches of salt. Cook, stirring frequently, until the chard is wilted.

3. **Season the ricotta for the filling.**

Put the ricotta, basil, nutritional yeast, miso, and 2 cloves of the garlic in a medium bowl and mix well. Season with salt and pepper to taste and add more garlic if desired.

4. **Preheat the oven.**

Preheat the oven to 400 degrees F. Line a baking sheet with parchment paper.

FILLING

3 tablespoons water

6 to 8 cloves garlic, minced

1 large bunch Swiss chard, coarsely chopped

Salt

1½ cups Almond Ricotta (page 47) or Macadamia Ricotta (page 19)

1 cup slivered fresh basil leaves, lightly packed

2 tablespoons nutritional yeast flakes

1 teaspoon medium brown miso

Ground pepper

1½ cups marinara sauce

5. **Shape the dough.**

When the dough has doubled in bulk, deflate it by punching it down all over with a fist. Turn it out onto a lightly floured work surface and knead a few times. Cut it into two equal pieces, then divide each half into four equal pieces. Shape each piece into a ball, then roll each into a circle about ¼ inch thick and 6 to 7 inches in diameter.

6. **Assemble the calzones.**

Leaving a ½-inch border all around, spread about 3 tablespoons of ricotta on one side of the circle, then top with one-eighth of the chard. Spread about 3 tablespoons of marinara sauce on top of the chard. Fold the dough over the filling to encase it completely, then press the edges together. Crimp the edges together all the way around (except along the fold) with the tines of a fork to ensure a secure seal. Using a small, sharp knife, make 3 to 4 slits on top of each calzone to allow steam to escape.

7. **Bake the calzones.**

Put the calzones on the lined baking sheet, arranging them so they aren't touching. Bake for about 20 minutes, until golden brown. Let cool for a minute or two before serving.

NOTE: Vital wheat gluten is pure gluten that's extracted from wheat and then dried and ground. Adding just a small amount of it when using alternative flours can help create more structure and a better rise in baked goods, and creates a lighter, crisper crust. It's generally available at natural food stores or with the natural foods in well-stocked supermarkets.

The first time I went to Greece, over thirty years ago, I practically lived on this classic dish in which spinach and cheese are encased in flaky phyllo pastry. Here's a vegan version with Tofu Feta that will transport you to the Greek Isles. The addition of fresh dill is an unusual twist, but it complements the spinach beautifully and adds another layer of flavor.

SPANAKOPITA

MAKES 6 TO 8 SERVINGS

1 pound regular or baby spinach

2 tablespoons extra-virgin olive oil or water

1 onion, finely chopped

3 cloves garlic, minced

1 small bunch (about ½ ounce) fresh dill, stemmed and minced (about ⅓ cup)

4 ounces Tofu Feta (page 25)

¼ cup pine nuts

Salt

Ground pepper

8 ounces phyllo dough, thawed

½ cup extra-virgin olive oil, or olive oil spray

1. **Prepare the spinach.**

   If using regular spinach, wash well, then drain and trim. To remove excess moisture, dry it in a salad spinner or gently blot it with a clean kitchen towel, then coarsely chop. If using baby spinach, rinse lightly, then drain and dry in a salad spinner or towel; there's no need to chop it.

2. **Cook the vegetables.**

   Heat the oil in a large skillet over medium heat. Add the onion and garlic and cook, stirring frequently, until tender, about 7 minutes. Add the spinach and dill and cook just until the spinach is wilted but still vibrant green, about 3 minutes. The longer you cook the spinach, the more water it will exude, so it's best to cook it only briefly. Transfer to a fine-mesh sieve and use the back of a wooden spoon to lightly press to expel excess liquid.

3. **Mix the filling.**

   Transfer the spinach mixture to a large bowl and crumble in the Tofu Feta. Add the pine nuts and mix well. Season with salt and pepper to taste.

4. **Assemble and bake.**

   Preheat the oven to 350 degrees F. Lightly brush or spray a 9- or 10-inch pie pan with oil. Unfold the stack of phyllo sheets on a clean, dry towel and cover with another clean, dry towel to keep the phyllo from drying out and getting brittle. Put one sheet of the phyllo on a dry surface and brush or spray lightly with the oil.

Per serving (based on 7 servings): calories: 350, protein: 9 g, fat: 25 g, saturated fat: 3 g, carbohydrate: 24 g, sodium: 261 mg, calcium: 122 mg

Phyllo dough can seem intimidating to work with, but it's actually quite easy to use. The key is to defrost it in the refrigerator overnight before attempting to unfold it and separate the sheets. The main recipe here yields one large pie, but you can also make individual portions of varying sizes, from entrée-sized to smaller, appetizer-sized morsels (see notes).

Repeat with the remaining of phyllo, stacking the sheets. Transfer the stack of phyllo sheets to the pie pan and press it into the pan, allowing the excess to hang over the side. Put the filling in the phyllo shell and spread it in an even layer. Fold the overhanging edges of the phyllo neatly over the top. Bake for 45 to 60 minutes, until puffy and golden brown.

NOTES: You can also shape the Spanakopita into individual entrée-sized portions or smaller portions for appetizers.

- For entrée-sized portions, cut the stack of unoiled phyllo sheets in half lengthwise to form two stacks, each measuring about 16 x 6 inches. Work with one stack and keep the other covered with a dry towel. Put one strip of phyllo on a dry surface and lightly brush or spray with oil. Repeat with two more strips of phyllo to make a stack with three layers. Put about ½ cup of filling about 3 inches up from the end of the strip. Fold the end of the strip diagonally over the filling to form a triangle, then lightly brush or spray oil on the folded-over portion. Fold repeatedly like a flag, flipping the triangle over and over again until you reach the end of the strip, making a neat parcel. Set the triangle on a lightly oiled baking sheet, seam-side down. Brush or spray with oil. Repeat with the remaining phyllo and filling.

- For appetizers, use the same method as for entrée-sized triangles, but fold each strip of phyllo in half lengthwise after brushing or spraying with oil, forming a strip about 3 inches wide. Use about 2 tablespoons of the filling for each triangle.

In traditional versions of this Mexican dish, the stuffed chiles are typically deep-fried. Here, I offer two options: a more traditional fried version, and a variation for a lighter version that's baked. Be aware that handling even mild chiles can make your hands burn—or make your eyes or other sensitive areas burn if you touch them after handling the chiles. To protect yourself, rub a little oil on your hands before working with the chiles.

CHILES RELLENOS with ranchero sauce

MAKES 6 SERVINGS

SAUCE

2 to 3 dried red New Mexico chiles or other medium-heat dried red chiles

2 cups boiling water

½ onion, cut into quarters

6 tablespoons unbleached flour

2 tablespoons cacao nibs

2 cloves garlic

½ teaspoon salt, plus more as desired

¼ teaspoon ground cinnamon

¼ teaspoon ground cumin

2 cups vegan chicken broth

1. **Reconstitute the dried chiles for the sauce.**
   Put the dried chiles in a large bowl and pour the boiling water over them. Let soak for 1 hour. Drain, reserving the soaking liquid, and remove the tops of the chiles. For a very mild sauce, make a slit in the peppers, scrape out the seeds, and discard them.

2. **Process the sauce ingredients.**
   Put the chiles, the reserved soaking water, and the onion, flour, cacao nibs, garlic, salt, cinnamon, and cumin in a blender and process until smooth.

3. **Cook the sauce.**
   Pour the dried chile mixture into a heavy medium saucepan and stir in the broth. Bring to a simmer over medium heat. Decrease the heat to medium-low and simmer, stirring occasionally, until thick enough to coat the back of a wooden spoon, about 10 minutes. Taste and add more salt if desired.

4. **Stuff the roasted chiles.**
   Working carefully to keep the roasted chiles intact with their tops in place, remove their skins. Cut a lengthwise slit in each chile and carefully scrape out the seeds and membranes through the slit. Put a slice of the cheese in each chile. Close the slit, overlapping the edges slightly.

Per serving: calories: 347, protein: 5 g, fat: 21 g, saturated fat: 2 g, carbohydrate: 35 g, sodium: 806 mg, calcium: 75 mg

CHILES AND CHEESE

12 roasted Anaheim or poblano chiles
(see sidebar, page 77), left whole

1 pound Meltable Monterey Jack
(page 42 , Meltable Cheddar (page 43),
or Meltable Muenster (page 41), sliced
into 12 pieces a bit smaller than the
size of the chiles

BATTER AND OIL

½ cup sparkling water

2 tablespoons Ener-G egg replacer
(see page 134)

½ cup unbleached flour

½ cup canola or grapeseed oil

5. Make the batter.

Put the sparkling water and egg replacer in a medium bowl and whisk until well blended. Add the flour and whisk until well mixed.

6. Dip and fry the chiles.

Heat the oil in a large heavy frying pan until a drop of batter sizzles when dropped in the pan. Dip a chile in the batter, then let the excess batter drip off. Carefully put the chile in the oil and fry, carefully turning once, until browned and crispy on both sides, about 4 minutes. Keep adding chiles, but don't overcrowd the skillet. Drain briefly on paper towels. Serve immediately, pouring about ⅓ cup of the sauce over each chile.

VARIATION: To make a low-fat version that's still delectable, bake the stuffed chiles, omitting the batter. Preheat the oven to 350 degrees F. Spread 1 cup of the sauce evenly in a 13 x 9-inch baking pan, then arrange the stuffed chiles atop the sauce. Pour the remaining sauce evenly over the chiles. Bake uncovered for about 20 minutes, until the cheese is melted and the sauce is hot and bubbling.

These tasty burgers with a Southwestern flavor are great either on or off a bun. You can cook them in a skillet or in the oven. If you'd like to grill them, it's best to bake them first to help keep them from falling apart. For the same reason, it's best to bake them first if you'd like to store them to serve later (see notes).

BLACK BEAN AND WILD RICE burgers

MAKES 10 TO 12 BURGERS

¼ cup water

1 onion, diced

2 stalks celery, diced

1 red bell pepper, diced

1 can (15 ounces) **black beans, drained**

4 to 6 ounces Sharp Cheddar (page 14), **coarsely chopped**

1 chipotle chile in adobo sauce

1 tablespoon medium brown miso

1 tablespoon tomato paste

1 clove garlic, coarsely chopped

2½ cups cooked wild rice (see notes)

½ cup panko

½ cup fresh cilantro, chopped

Salt

Ground pepper

1. **Cook the vegetables.**
Heat the water in a medium skillet over medium heat. Add the onion, celery, and bell pepper and cook, stirring frequently, until crisp-tender, 3 to 5 minutes.

2. **Process the ingredients.**
Put the beans, cheese, chile, miso, tomato paste, and garlic in a food processor. Pulse until well combined and slightly chunky, not completely smooth.

3. **Form the burgers.**
Transfer to a large bowl. Add the cooked vegetables, wild rice, panko, and cilantro and mix well. Season with salt and pepper to taste. Shape into patties by hand.

4. **Cook the burgers.**
Cook the burgers right away, either on the stovetop or in the oven. To cook them on the stovetop, heat a large nonstick skillet over medium heat. Lightly brush or spray the skillet with oil. Cook until the underside is browned, about 7 minutes, then turn and cook until the other side is browned, about 5 to 7 minutes longer. To bake them, preheat the oven to 350 degrees F and line a baking sheet with parchment paper. Put the patties on the lined baking sheet and bake for about 20 minutes, until browned and firm.

Per serving (based on 6 servings): calories: 175, protein: 8 g, fat: 5 g, saturated fat: 1 g, carbohydrate: 22 g, sodium: 170 mg, calcium: 23 mg

NOTES: Wild rice takes a long time to cook, so you'll need to prepare it in advance. Here are some tips you may find helpful for making and storing Black Bean and Wild Rice Burgers.

- To cook the wild rice, put 1 cup of wild rice and 4 cups of water in a medium saucepan. Cover and bring to a boil over high heat. Decrease the heat to low and cook for 50 to 60 minutes, until the grains are split. Remove from the heat and let steam for 15 minutes. Drain well. This may yield a bit more than 2½ cups of cooked wild rice; if so, enjoy the remainder as is or add it to a soup or stew.

- To store the baked burgers, wrap them tightly in plastic wrap. They will keep in the refrigerator for about 1 week or in the freezer for about 6 weeks. Thaw before cooking on a grill, frying in a skillet, or reheating in the oven.

This homey and comforting gratin with its creamy sauce and cheesy topping will please all diners, even those who previously thought they didn't like cauliflower.

CAULIFLOWER gratin

MAKES 6 SERVINGS AS AN ENTRÉE,
OR 8 TO 10 SERVINGS AS A SIDE DISH

1 tablespoon oil

1 onion, diced

1 large head cauliflower, cut into bite-sized florets

Salt

Ground pepper

2 cups water

¾ cup raw cashews

4 ounces Meltable Cheddar (page 43), Hard Gruyère (page 13), or Air-Dried Cheddar (page 30), sliced ¼ inch thick

1. **Preheat the oven.**
   Preheat the oven to 425 degrees F.

2. **Cook the vegetables.**
   Heat the oil in a large skillet over medium-high heat. Add the onion and cook, stirring frequently, just until tender, about 5 minutes. Add the cauliflower and season with salt and pepper. Cook, stirring frequently, until the cauliflower is slightly browned but still crisp-tender, about 5 minutes. Transfer to a 10 x 7-inch baking pan.

3. **Make the cashew sauce.**
   Put the water, cashews, and ½ teaspoon of salt in a blender. Process until smooth and creamy.

4. **Assemble and bake.**
   Pour the cashew sauce evenly over the cauliflower. Arrange the cheese slices on top. Bake for 25 to 30 minutes, until the sauce is thick and bubbling and the cheese is melted and browned.

Per serving (based on 6 servings): calories: 209, protein: 7 g, fat: 14 g, saturated fat: 2 g, carbohydrate: 13 g, sodium: 182 mg, calcium: 45 mg

We all need comfort food, and this is one of the favorites at my house (including among all of my kids' friends who eat here). Thinly sliced potatoes are layered with a rich cashew sauce, topped with cheese, and baked until slightly crisp. The result is a dish that's a fabulous brunch offering and can also be served as an entrée, accompanied by a big green salad. I guarantee that no one will be able to tell this isn't loaded with cream and dairy-based cheese!

POTATOES gratin

MAKES 6 TO 8 SERVINGS AS AN ENTRÉE, OR 12 TO 16 SERVINGS AS A SIDE DISH

4 cups water

1½ cups raw cashews, soaked in water for 2 to 3 hours and drained

1½ teaspoons salt

¼ teaspoon ground pepper

¼ teaspoon freshly grated nutmeg (optional)

3 to 4 pounds Yukon gold or other waxy potatoes, peeled and thinly sliced

8 to 12 ounces Meltable Cheddar (page 49), sliced ¼ inch thick

½ cup minced fresh chives (optional)

1. **Make the cashew sauce.**

   Put the water, cashews, salt, pepper, and optional nutmeg in a blender. Process until smooth and creamy.

2. **Assemble and bake.**

   Preheat the oven to 425 degrees F. Lightly brush or spray a 13 x 9-inch baking pan with oil. Neatly layer half of the potatoes in the pan, overlapping them slightly. Arrange about one-third of the cheese slices on top. Repeat with the remaining potatoes, then distribute the remaining cheese on top of the potatoes. Scatter the optional chives evenly over the cheese, then pour the cashew sauce evenly over the top. Cover and bake for about 40 minutes. Uncover and bake for 15 to 20 minutes, until the potatoes are tender, the sauce is thick and bubbling, and the cheese is melted and browned.

Per serving (based on 10 servings): calories: 425, protein: 13 g, fat: 22 g, saturated fat: 3 g, carbohydrate: 45 g, sodium: 455 mg, calcium: 43 mg

9

Sweet Cheese Dishes and Desserts

Cashew Cream Cheese, Mascarpone, and Almond Ricotta star in the fabulous creations in this chapter, which is filled with enticing cheese-inspired desserts and sweet breakfast or brunch dishes. Whether you're looking for decadent cheesecakes, classic tiramisu, or another glorious ending to your meal, or a special cheese-laced breakfast, such as fluffy blueberry pancakes with ricotta or showstopping blintzes, you will find a recipe for it here. Go ahead and indulge!

When first made the Raspberry Swirl Cheesecake (page 115), I couldn't stop eating the raspberry cheese-cake mixture, so I thought it would be great to use it as the basis for a mousse. Before making this recipe, be sure to read the details about chilled coconut cream on page 59. Also, be forewarned that you can't use light coconut milk to make the coconut cream, and that you'll need to refrigerate the coconut milk in the cans for at least twenty-four hours for the magic to happen.

RASPBERRY mousse

MAKES 8 SERVINGS

1¼ cups Cashew Cream Cheese
(page 55)

12 ounces fresh or frozen raspberries

½ cup agave nectar or sugar, plus
more as desired

1 teaspoon grated lemon zest

1 tablespoon freshly squeezed
lemon juice

1¼ cups chilled coconut cream
(see note, page 59)

½ cup water

1 teaspoon agar powder,
or 1 tablespoon agar flakes

1 cup fresh raspberries, for garnish

1. **Process the ingredients.**
Put the cream cheese, the 12 ounces of raspberries, and the agave nectar, lemon zest, and lemon juice in a food processor or blender. Process until smooth and creamy. Taste and add more agave nectar if desired. Leave the mixture in the food processor.

2. **Whip the coconut cream.**
Put the coconut cream in a chilled bowl. Using a handheld mixer or a stand mixer fitted with the whisk attachment, beat the coconut cream until soft peaks form, about 3 minutes.

3. **Dissolve the agar.**
Put the water and agar in a small saucepan and bring to a boil over medium-high heat. Decrease the heat to medium-low and simmer, whisking occasionally, until the agar is completely dissolved, 3 to 5 minutes. It should not be cloudy or grainy.

4. **Mix the mousse.**
Pour the dissolved agar into the food processor and process until thoroughly combined. Immediately pour the mixture into the whipped coconut cream. Mix on low speed or with a wire whisk to gently fold in the cream cheese mixture. Spoon into eight wine glasses or other individual dishes, decorate with the fresh raspberries, and refrigerate for at least 3 hours, until set.

LOW-FAT RASPBERRY MOUSSE: Instead of using chilled coconut cream, substitute 2 cups of whipped Flaxseed Meringue (page 120). This version will be fluffier, sweeter, and lighter.

Per serving: calories: 269, protein: 6 g, fat: 15 g, saturated fat: 5 g, carbohydrate: 28 g, sodium: 15 mg, calcium: 30 mg

This is my go-to raw crust for cheesecakes and other desserts. It's as easy to make as a graham cracker crust and just as tasty, but much more healthful—and gluten-free.

ALMOND-DATE crust

MAKES ONE 9-INCH CRUST

1 cup raw almonds

10 to 12 pitted dates

2 teaspoons vanilla extract

1. **Process the ingredients.**

   Put all the ingredients in a food processor. Process until crumbly, sticky, and thoroughly combined.

2. **Pat into the pan.**

   Transfer to a 9-inch springform pan and press the mixture in an even layer over the bottom of the pan.

Per ⅛ crust: calories: 144, protein: 4 g, fat: 9 g, saturated fat: 1 g, carbohydrate: 9 g, sodium: 1 mg, calcium: 54 mg

This simple crust is a snap to put together and provides an excellent base for cheesecakes. As a bonus, it's gluten-free. Although the recipe specifies an eight-inch springform pan, it will also work just fine to press the mixture into a nine-inch springform pan.

WALNUT-OAT CRUMBLE crust

MAKES ONE 8-INCH CRUST

½ cup old-fashioned rolled oats

½ cup walnuts

⅓ cup brown rice flour

¼ cup canola oil

2 to 3 tablespoons maple syrup

1. **Mix the ingredients.**
Put the oats, walnuts, and flour in a food processor. Process briefly, just until sandy in texture. Transfer to a bowl and stir in the oil. Add 2 tablespoons of the maple syrup and stir until the mixture comes together. If it doesn't hold together, add more maple syrup, 1 teaspoon at a time, until it does. The mixture shouldn't be wet.

2. **Pat into the pan.**
Brush or spray an 8-inch springform pan with oil. Transfer the mixture to the pan and press it in an even layer over the bottom of the pan and about ½ inch up the sides.

Per ⅛ crust: calories: 191, protein: 3 g, fat: 12 g, saturated fat: 1 g, carbohydrate: 17 g , sodium: 2 mg, calcium: 15 mg

When you don't have time to make Cashew Cream Cheese (page 20) for a cheesecake, here's a quick, creamy tart that's just as delightful as a cheesecake but without the sharp flavor that comes from cultured cheese. That's okay, because there are a lot of flavors going on here, from the crunchy almond crust to the sweet and creamy cheesy filling to the strawberries, both fresh in the tart and lightly cooked in a glistening glaze. Best of all, this indulgence is relatively healthful; aside from the small amount of sweetener used, it's basically just fruit and nuts.

creamy STRAWBERRY TART

MAKES ONE 9-INCH TART (12 SERVINGS)

FILLING

3½ cups water

1½ cups raw cashews

½ cup agave nectar or sugar

2 tablespoons arrowroot starch or tapioca flour

Grated zest of 2 lemons

1 to 2 tablespoons freshly squeezed lemon juice

1 teaspoon vanilla extract

½ cup water

1 teaspoon agar powder, or 1 tablespoon agar flakes

1. **Combine the filling ingredients.**
Put the water and cashews in a blender and process until smooth and creamy. Add the agave nectar, arrowroot, lemon zest, 1 tablespoon of the lemon juice, and the vanilla extract. Process until thoroughly combined. Taste and add more lemon juice if desired.

2. **Cook the filling.**
Pour the cashew mixture into a large heavy saucepan over medium-low heat. Cook, stirring frequently, until very thick and goopy, about 5 minutes. Cover and remove from the heat.

3. **Thicken the filling.**
Immediately, before the filling cools, put the water and agar in a small saucepan and bring to a boil over medium-high heat. Decrease the heat to medium-low and simmer, whisking occasionally, until the agar is completely dissolved, 3 to 5 minutes. It should not be cloudy or grainy. Pour the hot mixture into the saucepan with the cashew mixture and whisk briskly until smooth and entirely free of lumps.

4. **Chill the filling in the tart crust.**
Pour the filling into the crust, spread it in an even layer, and smooth the top. Let cool at room temperature, then cover and refrigerate for about 1 hour, until the top is firm enough to hold the strawberries.

Per serving: calories: 294, protein: 7 g, fat: 15 g, saturated fat: 2 g, carbohydrate: 34 g, sodium: 4 mg, calcium: 57 mg

CRUST AND STRAWBERRIES

1 Almond-Date Crust (page 108)

2 pints strawberries (see note), **hulled**

GLAZE

1 pint strawberries, hulled

¼ cup agave nectar or sugar

2 tablespoons water

1½ tablespoons arrowroot starch
or tapioca flour

5. Decorate with strawberries.

Arrange the 2 pints of strawberries decoratively atop the filling. (If they are large, cut them in half lengthwise; otherwise, you can leave them whole if you like.)

6. Blend the strawberries for the glaze.

Put the 1 pint of strawberries and the agave nectar in a blender and process briefly at low speed, just until relatively smooth. (Processing at low speed minimizes the amount of air mixed in, resulting in a glaze with a deeper red color. If the mixture becomes pink and frothy, you can set it aside until it settles and becomes redder, about 1 hour.)

7. Thicken the glaze and apply to the tart.

Transfer the blended strawberries to a medium saucepan over medium heat. Cook, stirring frequently, until hot but not bubbling. Combine the water and arrowroot in a small bowl and stir to form a smooth paste. Add to the strawberry mixture and cook, whisking frequently, until slightly thickened and glossy, 1 to 2 minutes. Pour the hot glaze evenly over the tart. Let the tart cool briefly at room temperature, then cover and refrigerate for at least 2 hours, until completely chilled before serving.

NOTE: In order to make the tart as visually appealing as possible, go through all 3 pints of strawberries—the 2 pints for the filling and the 1 pint for the glaze—and select the berries that are most uniform in size to equal 2 pints. Use those to fill the tart crust, and use the remaining pint of odd-sized berries for the glaze.

Traditional no-bake cheesecakes are usually made with gelatin. Both this recipe and the Fluffy No-Bake Cheesecake (page 113) use agar to help the filling set. This version is creamy and somewhat dense, harkening back to memories of classic cheesecake with a graham cracker crust. Easy to make and absolutely delightful, this dessert is hard to beat. For the crust, you can substitute a traditional graham cracker crust, but the Almond-Date Crust is more healthful and, I think, tastier.

creamy NO-BAKE CHEESECAKE

See photo facing page 119.

MAKES ONE 9-INCH CHEESECAKE (16 SERVINGS)

5 cups Cashew Cream Cheese (page 20)

1 cup sugar

1 cup maple syrup

Grated zest and juice of 2 lemons

1 tablespoon vanilla extract

1½ cups water

2 tablespoons agar powder, or 6 tablespoons agar flakes

1 Almond-Date Crust (page 108)

1. **Process the filling ingredients.**

   Combine the cream cheese, sugar, maple syrup, lemon zest and juice, and vanilla extract in a 12- to 14-cup food processor (see note). Process until smooth and creamy. Leave the mixture in the food processor.

2. **Dissolve the agar.**

   Put the water and agar in a small saucepan and bring to a boil over medium-high heat. Decrease the heat to medium-low and simmer until the agar is completely dissolved, 3 to 5 minutes. It should not be cloudy or grainy.

3. **Mix the filling.**

   Pour the dissolved agar into the food processor and process until thoroughly combined with the cream cheese mixture.

4. **Assemble and chill the cheesecake.**

   Pour the filling into the crust, spread it in an even layer, and smooth the top. Cover and refrigerate for at least 4 hours, until firm enough to slice.

   NOTE: If you don't have a large-capacity food processor, you will need to mash all the filling ingredients in a large bowl and process the mixture in batches.

Per serving: calories: 440, protein: 11 g, fat: 26 g, saturated fat: 4 g, carbohydrate: 44 g, sodium: 32 mg, calcium: 72 mg

This no-bake cheesecake is not only creamy but also light and fluffy, thanks to whipped coconut cream. If you like, pile some fresh berries on top before digging in! Before making this recipe, be sure to read the details about chilled coconut cream on page 59.

FLUFFY NO-BAKE cheesecake

MAKES ONE 9-INCH CHEESECAKE
(12 SERVINGS)

2½ cups Cashew Cream Cheese
(page 20)

½ cup sugar

½ cup maple syrup

Grated zest and juice of 2 lemons

2 teaspoons vanilla extract

1¼ cups chilled coconut cream
(see note, page 59)

¾ cup water

1 tablespoon agar powder,
or 3 tablespoons agar flakes

1 Almond-Date Crust (page 108)

1. **Process the cream cheese.**
   Combine the cream cheese, sugar, maple syrup, lemon zest and juice, and vanilla extract in a food processor. Process until smooth and creamy. Leave the mixture in the food processor.

2. **Whip the coconut cream.**
   Put the coconut cream in a chilled bowl. Using a handheld mixer or a stand mixer fitted with the whisk attachment, beat the coconut cream until soft peaks form, about 3 minutes.

3. **Dissolve the agar.**
   Put the water and agar in a small saucepan and bring to a boil over medium-high heat. Decrease the heat to medium-low and simmer, whisking occasionally, until the agar is completely dissolved, 3 to 5 minutes. It should not be cloudy or grainy.

4. **Combine the agar and cream cheese mixture.**
   Pour the agar mixture into the food processor and process until thoroughly combined. Immediately pour the mixture into the whipped coconut cream. Mix on low speed or with a wire whisk to gently fold in the cream cheese mixture.

5. **Assemble and chill the cheesecake.**
   Pour the filling into the crust, spread it in an even layer, and smooth the top. Cover and refrigerate for at least 4 hours, until firm enough to slice.

Per serving: calories: 376, protein: 9 g, fat: 23 g, saturated fat: 6 g, carbohydrate: 34 g, sodium: 20 mg, calcium: 63 mg

This is actually a New York–style cheesecake, with a dense, rich filling. But because I live in San Francisco, and because the ingredients are decidedly untraditional (something San Franciscans embrace!), I call it a San Francisco Cheesecake. Serve it as is, or adorn it with berries, other fruit, or Fluffy Whipped Coconut Cream (page 59).

SAN FRANCISCO cheesecake

MAKES ONE 8-INCH CHEESECAKE (16 SERVINGS)

4 cups Cashew Cream Cheese (page 20)

1½ cups coconut milk, regular or light

10 ounces medium-firm regular or silken tofu

1 cup sugar

⅓ cup maple syrup, plus more as desired

3 tablespoons cornstarch

2 tablespoons brandy

Grated zest of 1 lemon

2 tablespoons freshly squeezed lemon juice, plus more as desired

2 teaspoons vanilla extract

1 teaspoon agar powder, or 1 tablespoon agar flakes

¼ teaspoon salt

1 Walnut-Oat Crumble Crust (page 109)

1. Preheat the oven.
Preheat the oven to 350 degrees F.

2. Make the filling.
Combine the cream cheese, coconut milk, tofu, sugar, maple syrup, cornstarch, brandy, lemon zest, lemon juice, vanilla extract, agar, and salt in a 12- to 14-cup food processor (see note). Process until smooth and creamy. Taste and stir in more maple syrup or lemon juice if desired.

3. Bake the cheesecake.
Pour the filling into the prepared crust, spread it in an even layer, and smooth the top. Bake for about 1 hour and 15 minutes, until the top has puffed up and is dry to the touch; it may have a few cracks. Let the cheesecake cool completely at room temperature. Cover and refrigerate for at least 10 hours, until firm enough to slice.

NOTE: If you don't have a large-capacity food processor, you will need to mash all the ingredients in a large bowl and process the mixture in batches.

Per serving: calories: 429, protein: 10 g, fat: 28 g, saturated fat: 7 g, carbohydrate: 37 g, sodium: 63 mg, calcium: 37 mg

Puréed raspberries add both visual appeal and a refreshing flavor to this cheesecake.

RASPBERRY SWIRL cheesecake

**MAKES ONE 8-INCH CHEESECAKE
(14 SERVINGS)**

3¼ cups Cashew Cream Cheese
(page 20)

1 can (13.5 ounces) coconut milk

1 cup sugar

¼ cup cornstarch

2 tablespoons Ener-G egg replacer
(see page 134)

2 teaspoons grated lemon zest

2 tablespoons freshly squeezed
lemon juice

1 tablespoon vanilla extract

1 Walnut-Oat Crumble Crust
(page 109)

6 ounces fresh or frozen raspberries

1. **Preheat the oven.**
   Preheat the oven to 350 degrees F.

2. **Make the filling.**
   Put the cream cheese, coconut milk, sugar, cornstarch, egg replacer, lemon zest, lemon juice, and vanilla extract in a food processor. Process until smooth and creamy. Set ½ cup of the mixture aside. Pour the rest of the filling into the crust, spread it in an even layer, and smooth the top.

3. **Make the raspberry swirl.**
   Put the reserved ½ cup of the cream cheese mixture back in the food processor and add the raspberries. Process until creamy and pink. Drop tablespoons of the mixture over the filling and use a knife to swirl it into the top of the filling to create an attractive pink design.

4. **Bake the cheesecake.**
   Bake the cheesecake for about 50 minutes, until the top has puffed up and is dry to the touch but the center is still wobbly. Let the cheesecake cool completely at room temperature. Cover and refrigerate for at least 8 hours, until firm enough to slice.

Per serving: calories: 431, protein: 8 g, fat: 28 g, saturated fat: 8 g, carbohydrate: 38 g, sodium: 23 mg, calcium: 30 mg

If you're tired of pumpkin pie at holiday time, give this festive cheesecake a spin. Although you can use any crust you like, including Almond-Date Crust (page 108) or Walnut-Oat Crumble Crust (page 109), the slightly spiced shortbread crust in this recipe complements the pumpkin perfectly.

PUMPKIN cheesecake

**MAKES ONE 9-INCH CHEESECAKE
(12 SERVINGS)**

CRUST

¾ cup finely ground almonds
(see notes)

½ cup whole wheat pastry flour

⅓ cup rolled oats

3 tablespoons evaporated cane juice
or coconut sugar

1 teaspoon ground cinnamon

½ teaspoon ground nutmeg

Pinch salt

6 tablespoons canola oil (see notes)

2 tablespoons brandy, dark rum,
apple juice, or water, plus more as
needed

1. **Preheat the oven.**

   Preheat the oven to 350 degrees F. Brush or spray a 9-inch spring-form pan with oil.

2. **Make the crust.**

   Put the almonds, flour, oats, sugar, cinnamon, nutmeg, and salt in a medium bowl and mix well. Drizzle the oil over the top and mix with a fork until crumbly. Stir in the brandy and gather into a ball. If the mixture doesn't stick together or looks dry, add a few additional drops of brandy or water. Transfer to the prepared pan and press in an even layer over the bottom of the pan.

3. **Make the filling.**

   Put the pumpkin, tofu, sugar, and maple syrup in a 12- to 14-cup food processor (see notes) and process until smooth and creamy. Add the cream cheese, tapioca flour, optional orange zest, cinnamon, agar, ginger, vanilla extract, salt, and nutmeg. Process again smooth and creamy.

4. **Bake the cheesecake.**

   Pour the filling into the prepared crust, spread it in an even layer, and smooth the top. Bake for 1 to 1¼ hours, until the top has puffed up and is dry to the touch; it may have a few cracks. Let the cheesecake cool completely at room temperature. Cover and refrigerate for at least 8 hours, until firm enough to slice.

Per serving: calories: 451, protein: 11 g, fat: 24 g, saturated fat: 3 g, carbohydrate: 47 g, sodium: 136 mg, calcium: 105 mg

FILLING

1 can (15 ounces) **pumpkin purée**

10 ounces **medium-firm or firm regular tofu**

¾ cup **sugar**

¾ cup **maple syrup**

2 cups **Cashew Cream Cheese** (page 20)

⅓ cup **tapioca flour or cornstarch**

Grated **zest of 1 orange** (optional)

2 teaspoons **ground cinnamon**

1 teaspoon **agar powder,** or 1 tablespoon **agar flakes**

1 teaspoon **ground ginger,** or 2 teaspoons **peeled and grated fresh ginger**

1 teaspoon **vanilla extract**

½ teaspoon **salt**

½ teaspoon **ground nutmeg**

NOTES: Here are some tips you may find helpful when making Pumpkin Cheesecake.

- Either blanched almonds or almonds with skins can be used for the crust.

- If possible, put the oil in the freezer for 45 minutes before making the crust; this will firm it up and result in a flakier crust.

- If you don't have a large-capacity food processor, you will need to mash all the ingredients in a large bowl and process the mixture in batches.

Rich, delicious, and chocolaty, with the perfect amount of tangy bite from the homemade cream cheese and enhanced by a hazelnut crust, this cheesecake is quite addicting.

CHOCOLATE cheesecake

MAKES ONE 8- OR 9-INCH CHEESECAKE (16 SERVINGS)

CRUST

¾ cup hazelnuts

⅓ cup brown rice flour or whole wheat pastry flour

⅓ cup evaporated cane juice or sugar

⅓ cup unsweetened cocoa powder

3 tablespoons canola oil

1 to 2 tablespoons brandy, rum, or water

FILLING

3¼ cups Cashew Cream Cheese (page 20)

1 cup evaporated cane juice or sugar

1½ cups coconut milk

12 ounces dark or semisweet chocolate, melted (see notes)

½ cup maple syrup

3 tablespoons cornstarch

1 tablespoon Ener-G egg replacer (see page 134)

1 tablespoon vanilla extract

1. **Preheat the oven and prepare the pan.**
Preheat the oven to 350 degrees F. Line the bottom of an 8- or 9-inch springform pan with a round of parchment paper. Generously brush or spray the bottom and sides with oil.

2. **Make the crust.**
Put the hazelnuts, flour, evaporated cane juice, and cocoa powder in a food processor and process until the hazelnuts are finely ground but not oily. Add the oil and process briefly, just until the dry ingredients are moistened. Add 1 tablespoon of the brandy and process briefly. Squeeze a bit of the mixture between your fingers to see if it's moist enough to stick together. If it isn't, add more brandy, 1 teaspoon at a time, processing briefly after each addition, until it holds together when squeezed. Transfer to the prepared pan and press it in an even layer over the bottom and about ½ inch up the sides.

3. **Make the filling.**
Put the cream cheese and evaporated cane juice in a food processor and process until creamy, fluffy, and lump-free. Add the coconut milk, melted chocolate, maple syrup, cornstarch, egg replacer, and vanilla extract and process until smooth and creamy.

4. **Bake the cheesecake.**
Pour the filling into the prepared crust, spread it in an even layer, and smooth the top. Bake for about 1 hour, until the top has puffed up and is dry to the touch; it may have a few cracks. Let the cheesecake cool completely at room temperature. Cover and refrigerate for at least 8 hours, until firm enough to slice. (continued on page 119)

Per serving: calories: 486, protein: 8 g, fat: 30 g, saturated fat: 9 g, carbohydrate: 48 g, sodium: 19 mg, calcium: 40 mg

Tiramisu, *page 120,* **Chocolate-Chestnut Cannoli,** *page 126*

Creamy No-Bake Cheesecake, *page 112*

NOTES: You can use the stove or the microwave to melt chocolate. Either way, do not let the chocolate get hot; as it melts, it should feel barely warm to the touch.

- If using block chocolate, coarsely chop it into ½-inch chunks, then put it in a glass bowl or the top of a double boiler. If using chocolate chips, simply put them in the bowl. Make sure that the bowl is completely dry; even a drop of water can cause the chocolate to become grainy.

- To use a microwave, put the chocolate in a glass bowl or measuring cup and microwave for no more than 1 minute at a time (and only about 30 seconds at a time for smaller quantities of chocolate). Check and stir well after every interval. Once the chocolate is almost completely melted, continue to stir until no chunks remain.

- To use a double boiler, put the chocolate in the top of a double boiler over barely simmering water; the water shouldn't touch the top part of the double boiler. Alternatively, put the chocolate in a glass or metal bowl and set it over a saucepan of barely simmering water. The bowl should fit snugly so that it traps the steam in the pot below; again, the water shouldn't touch the bottom of the bowl. Heat, stirring frequently, until the chocolate has melted on the bottom. Remove from the heat and continue to stir until melted and smooth.

This vegan take on a classic Italian dessert will have a truly authentic flavor when you start off with your own Mascarpone. To make the assembly easy, bake the ladyfingers a day or even a week in advance; just wrap them well and store them at room temperature. The flaxseed gel for the meringue can also be made up to a week in advance, but it should be whipped no more than two days before assembly of the tiramisu. Before making this recipe, be sure to read the details about chilled coconut cream on page 59.

TIRAMISU

See photo facing page 118.

MAKES 12 SERVINGS

LADYFINGERS

½ cup water

3 tablespoons Ener-G egg replacer (see page 134)

¼ cup sugar

¼ cup canola oil

4 tablespoons plain or vanilla soy milk

¾ cup unbleached flour or cake flour

1 teaspoon baking powder

FLAXSEED MERINGUE

3 cups water

⅓ cup flaxseeds

Per serving: calories: 417, protein: 7 g, fat: 23 g, saturated fat: 7 g, carbohydrate: 46 g, sodium: 62 mg, calcium: 58 mg

1. **Preheat the oven and prepare the pans.**
Preheat the oven to 350 degrees F. Line two rimmed baking sheets with parchment paper.

2. **Make the batter for the ladyfingers.**
Put the water and egg replacer in a small bowl and whisk vigorously until the mixture is thick and soft peaks form. Add the sugar and whisk until thoroughly incorporated, then add the oil and whisk vigorously until well blended. Add 2 tablespoons of the soy milk and whisk until well blended. Sift the flour and baking powder into a separate bowl. Add to the egg replacer mixture and gently fold in just until combined. Gently, so as not to deflate the mixture, stir in the remaining soy milk.

3. **Bake the ladyfingers.**
Spoon the mixture onto the lined baking sheets to make 20 oblong ladyfingers, each about 3 inches long and 1 inch wide, spacing them at least 1 inch apart. Bake for about 15 minutes, until firm but still white. Transfer to a wire rack and let cool completely.

4. **Cook the flaxseeds for the meringue.**
Combine the water and flaxseeds in a medium saucepan and bring to a boil over medium-high heat. Decrease the heat to medium-low and simmer, stirring occasionally, until thick and gelatinous about 20 minutes.

5. **Strain the flaxseed gel.**
Put a sieve over a small bowl. Strain the flaxseed mixture; there should be about ½ cup of very viscous, gooey gel in the bowl. Let cool completely at room temperature, then cover and refrigerate until chilled, about 30 minutes.

MASCARPONE CREAM

2 cups Mascarpone (page 21)

¼ cup water

1 teaspoon agar powder, or
1 tablespoon agar flakes

1¼ cups coconut cream (see note, page 59)

½ cup powdered sugar

1 tablespoon vanilla extract, plus more as desired

ESPRESSO SYRUP AND COCOA DUSTING

1¼ cups hot espresso or very strong coffee

¼ cup sugar

3 tablespoons brandy or coffee-flavored liqueur

2 to 3 tablespoons unsweetened cocoa powder, for dusting

6. **Whip the meringue.**

Using a handheld mixer or a stand mixer fitted with the whisk attachment, whip the flaxseed gel until light, fluffy, and white—much like beaten egg whites—7 to 8 minutes.

7. **Process the cream cheese for the mascarpone cream.**

Put the cream cheese in a food processor and process until creamy. Leave the mixture in the food processor.

8. **Dissolve the agar and combine with the cream cheese.**

Put the water and agar in a small saucepan and bring to a boil over medium-high heat. Decrease the heat to medium-low and simmer, stirring frequently with a whisk, until the agar is completely dissolved, 3 to 5 minutes. It should not be cloudy or grainy. Pour the dissolved agar into the food processor and process until thoroughly combined with the cream cheese. Transfer to a large bowl.

9. **Whip the coconut cream.**

Put the coconut cream in a chilled bowl. Using a handheld mixer or a stand mixer fitted with the whisk attachment, beat the coconut cream until soft peaks form, about 3 minutes.

10. **Make the mascarpone cream.**

Sift the powdered sugar into the bowl with the whipped coconut cream and add the vanilla extract. Mix on low speed just until incorporated. Scrape the whipped cream into the bowl with the cream cheese mixture and gently fold it in. Add the whipped meringue and gently fold it in. Taste and add more vanilla extract if desired.

11. **Make the espresso syrup.**

Combine the espresso and sugar in a small bowl and stir until the sugar is dissolved. Stir in the brandy.

12. **Assemble the tiramisu.**

Dip half of the ladyfingers in the espresso syrup, one at a time, allowing each to soak for about 3 seconds to absorb the syrup. Arrange them, slightly overlapping, in a 9-inch square pan. Spread half of the mascarpone cream gently and evenly over the ladyfingers. Soak the remaining ladyfingers in the espresso syrup in the same way, then arrange them, slightly overlapping, over the mascarpone cream. Spread the remaining mascarpone cream evenly over the ladyfingers and smooth the top. Using a sifter or fine-mesh sieve, dust the top with the cocoa powder. Cover and refrigerate for at least 6 hours before serving to allow the flavors to meld.

Here's a sweet and elegant alternative to pumpkin pie for the holidays. As a bonus, it can be made in advance and frozen for up to two months. Just thaw it in the refrigerator for one day before serving. Before making this recipe, be sure to read the details about chilled coconut cream on page 59.

PUMPKIN tiramisu

MAKES 16 SERVINGS

½ cup rum

2 tablespoons sugar or coconut sugar

20 ounces vegan gingersnaps

1¼ cups chilled coconut cream (see note, page 59)

1 can (15 ounces) pumpkin purée

1 cup Mascarpone (page 21)

¾ cup maple syrup, sugar, or coconut sugar

1 tablespoon ground cinnamon

1 teaspoon vanilla extract

½ cup water

2 teaspoons agar powder, or 2 tablespoons agar flakes

1. **Prepare the cookie crust.**
   Put the rum and sugar in a small saucepan over medium heat. Cook, stirring constantly, just until the sugar dissolves, 3 to 5 minutes. Line a 13 x 9-inch baking pan with 8 ounces of the gingersnaps. Brush half of the rum mixture over the cookies.

2. **Whip the coconut milk.**
   Put the coconut cream in a chilled bowl. Using a handheld mixer or a stand mixer fitted with the whisk attachment, beat the coconut cream until soft peaks form.

3. **Process the pumpkin and Mascarpone.**
   Put the pumpkin, Mascarpone, maple syrup, cinnamon, and vanilla extract in a blender or food processor. Process until smooth and creamy. Leave the mixture in the blender.

4. **Dissolve the agar.**
   Combine the water and agar in a small saucepan and bring to a boil over medium-high heat. Decrease the heat to medium-low and simmer, stirring frequently with a whisk, until the agar is completely dissolved, 3 to 5 minutes. It should not be cloudy or grainy.

Per serving: calories: 418, protein: 4 g, fat: 13 g, saturated fat: 7 g, carbohydrate: 65 g, sodium: 225 mg, calcium: 31 mg

5. Make the pumpkin filling.

Pour the dissolved agar into the blender and process until thoroughly combined with the pumpkin mixture. Transfer to a large bowl. Add about half of the whipped coconut cream and gently fold it in.

6. Assemble the tiramisu.

Spread half of the pumpkin filling over the rum-infused gingersnaps, then spread half of the remaining whipped coconut cream over the top. Arrange another 8 ounces of the gingersnaps evenly over the top and brush with the remaining rum mixture. Spread the remaining pumpkin filling over the gingersnaps, then spread the remaining coconut whipped cream on top. Crush the remaining 4 ounces of gingersnaps with a rolling pin to form crumbs. Sprinkle the crumbs evenly over the top. Cover and refrigerate for at least 6 hours before serving to allow the flavors to meld.

Frozen pineapple juice concentrate adds a refreshing tang to this carrot cake. If you like, you can add chopped fresh pineapple too. Walnuts, coconut, and raisins are other optional enhancements. Topped with cream cheese frosting, it is one of my all-time favorite desserts.

GOLDEN CARROT CAKE with cream cheese frosting

MAKES ONE 9-INCH DOUBLE-LAYER CAKE
(16 SERVINGS)

CREAM CHEESE FROSTING

2 cups Cashew Cream Cheese
(page 20)

1 cup refined coconut oil, melted
but not hot

1 cup maple syrup

1 teaspoon xanthan gum

1. **Make the frosting.**

   Put the cream cheese, oil, and maple syrup in a food processor. Process until smooth and creamy. Add the xanthan gum and process until thoroughly combined. Transfer to a container, cover, and refrigerate for at least 3 hours, until thickened, before frosting the cake.

2. **Preheat the oven and prepare the pans.**

   Preheat the oven to 350 degrees F. Line the bottoms of two 9-inch round cake pans with parchment paper and spray the sides with nonstick spray. Alternatively, oil the entire interior of the pans generously, then dust with flour.

Per serving: calories: 557, protein: 8 g, fat: 33 g, saturated fat: 14 g, carbohydrate: 58 g, sodium: 230 mg, calcium: 105 mg

CAKE

3 cups whole wheat pastry flour

1 tablespoon baking powder

2 teaspoons ground cinnamon

1 teaspoon baking soda

1 teaspoon salt

1 teaspoon ground cardamom

1 teaspoon ground ginger

1 cup sugar, coconut sugar,
or a combination

1 cup plain or vanilla almond milk
or soy milk

1 tablespoon cider vinegar

¾ cup canola oil

½ cup frozen concentrated pineapple
juice, thawed

¼ cup maple syrup

1 pound carrots, scrubbed and grated

1 cup chopped fresh pineapple (optional)

1 cup walnuts (optional), lightly toasted
(see note, page 69) and chopped

1 cup raisins or unsweetened
shredded dried coconut (optional)

3. Sift the dry ingredients.

Sift the flour, baking powder, cinnamon, baking soda, salt, cardamom, and ginger into a large bowl. Add the sugar and stir with a whisk to combine.

4. Combine the wet ingredients.

Combine the almond milk and vinegar in a separate large bowl and mix well. Let sit until thickened and slightly curdled, 2 to 3 minutes. Add the oil, juice concentrate, and maple syrup and whisk vigorously until thoroughly blended.

5. Make the batter.

Pour the flour mixture into the almond milk mixture and mix well with a wooden spoon. Add the carrots and the optional pineapple, walnuts, or raisins.

6. Bake the cake.

Divide the batter evenly between the two prepared pans. Bake for about 35 minutes, until golden brown and a toothpick inserted in the center of each cake comes out clean. Let cool completely at room temperature before turning out of the pans.

7. Frost the cake.

To assemble and frost the cake, put one cake on a large plate or round platter. Spread a thick layer of frosting over the top. Place the second cake layer on top. Spread about two-thirds of the remaining frosting over the sides of the cake, then spread the remaining frosting evenly over the top.

This dessert is, simply put, divinely delicious. The crisp shell holds a rich, creamy chocolate concoction, and the ends of the filled shells are dipped in chocolate for added decadence. It's hard to eat just one, but this is also the kind of dessert that makes you want to take your time and savor every bite.

In this rendition of the Italian classic, I use vegan wonton wrappers for the cannoli shells, which eases preparation. There are two tools I recommend for making these: cannoli tubes and a pastry bag. Cannoli

CHOCOLATE-CHESTNUT cannoli

See photo facing page 118.

MAKES 14 CANNOLI

FILLING

6 ounces peeled and cooked chestnuts (bottled, frozen, or vacuum-packed)

½ cup maple syrup

⅔ cup Cashew Cream Cheese (page 20)

⅔ cup Almond Ricotta (page 47)

3 ounces dark chocolate, melted (see notes, page 119)

2 tablespoons unsweetened cocoa powder

2 tablespoons rum

1 teaspoon vanilla extract

2 tablespoons cacao nibs

1. **Make the filling.**

Combine the chestnuts and maple syrup in a food processor and process until fairly creamy. Add the cream cheese, ricotta, melted chocolate, cocoa powder, rum, and vanilla extract and process until smooth, light, and creamy. Transfer to a bowl and stir in the cacao nibs.

2. **Heat the oil and check the oil temperature.**

Pour oil into a wok or wide pot to a depth of about 2 inches. Put the wok over medium heat. When the oil reaches about 375 degrees F, it's ready. If you don't have a kitchen thermometer, test the oil temperature by adding a small piece of one wrapper to it. If it sinks but rises quickly and steadily to the top, the oil is hot enough. If it sinks to the bottom and lingers there for a moment, the oil isn't yet hot enough. Having the oil at the right temperature is important to achieving a light, crispy texture.

3. **Fry the shells.**

Lightly brush or spray the cannoli tubes with oil. Wrap a wonton wrapper around the tube. Brush a bit of water along the overlapping edges and press lightly to seal. Carefully lower the shells (still on the tubes) into the oil and cook until golden brown, just 20 to 30 seconds. Remove with tongs, tipping each shell vertically so any oil inside the tube drains into the pot. Drain briefly on paper towels. Using a paper towel so you don't burn your fingers, slip the shell off of the tube. Repeat with the remaining wrappers.

Per cannoli: calories: 286, protein: 5 g, fat: 22 g, saturated fat: 6 g, carbohydrate: 19 g, sodium: 30 mg, calcium: 38 mg tubes are forms used to help the shells keep their shape during frying (or baking); I recommend that you have three or four of them. Both cannoli tubes and pastry bags are inexpensive and readily available online or at kitchen supply stores. However, you can improvise for both. In place of the cannoli tubes, use wooden dowels cut to three-inch lengths. As for the pastry bag, a gallon-sized plastic bag with one corner snipped off works perfectly well.

OIL, SHELLS, AND GARNISHES

Canola oil, for frying (3 to 4 cups, depending on the size of the pot)

14 vegan wonton or pot sticker wrappers

3 ounces dark chocolate, melted (see notes, page 119)

¼ cup powdered sugar (optional), **for sprinkling**

4. **Fill the shells.**

Put the filling in a pastry bag, filling it no more than half full. Use a large star or plain tip. Twist the bag above the filling, holding the bag where you have twisted it. Insert the tip into one end of a cannoli shell and squeeze to extrude the filling, then turn the shell 180 degrees and pipe filling into the other end to completely fill the shell. Repeat with the remaining shells and filling.

5. **Decorate the cannoli.**

Dip both ends of the filled cannoli in the melted chocolate. Put the dipped cannoli on a plate or wire rack and let sit until the chocolate sets. Using a sifter or fine-mesh sieve, dust the tops of the cannoli with the optional powdered sugar. Serve immediately, or store in a sealed container in the refrigerator for up to 2 hours.

These blintzes are delightfully decadent brunch fare, yet if you analyze the ingredients, you'll see that they consist primarily of healthful nuts, seeds, whole grains, and fruit. Sure, there's a little sweetener, but it comes in the form of maple syrup, and recent studies have indicated that this sweetener is packed with antioxidants and other nutrients.

BUCKWHEAT BLINTZES
with cream cheese and caramelized apples

MAKES 12 TO 14 BLINTZES

CRÊPES

2 cups water

¾ cup buckwheat flour

½ cup whole wheat pastry flour

¼ cup crumbled soft regular or soft silken tofu

3 tablespoons flaxseeds

1 teaspoon salt

1 teaspoon baking powder

1. **Make the crêpe batter.**

   Put the water, buckwheat flour, pastry flour, tofu, flaxseeds, salt, and baking powder in a blender. Process until smooth. Let the batter rest for 30 to 60 minutes before cooking; this will help the crêpes hold together better.

2. **Cook the crêpes.**

   Heat an 8-inch omelet or crêpe pan (see note) over medium heat. Very lightly brush or spray with oil. Stir the crêpe batter. Lift the pan off of the heat, pour in about ¼ cup of batter, and immediately tilt and swirl the pan to spread the batter over the entire bottom of the pan. Put the pan back on the burner and cook until the bottom of the crêpe is lightly browned, 1 to 2 minutes. Turn the crêpe and cook the other side until lightly browned, about 30 seconds. Repeat with the remaining batter, lightly brushing or spraying the pan with oil after cooking every two or three crêpes.

3. **Make the filling.**

   Put the cream cheese and maple syrup in a food processor and process until smooth and creamy.

4. **Fill the crêpes.**

   Put about ¼ cup of the cream cheese mixture in the center of a crêpe. Fold two opposite sides over the cheese, then fold in the other two sides to make a rectangular parcel. Repeat with the remaining crêpes and filling.

Per blintz (based on 13 blintzes): calories: 361, protein: 9 g, fat: 19 g, saturated fat: 3 g, carbohydrate: 41 g, sodium: 215 mg, calcium: 70 mg

The buckwheat flour gives the crêpes an appealing earthy flavor. They're extremely versatile and pair well with both sweet and savory fillings. For a fun and easy entrée, stuff them with almost any of the cheeses in this book and cooked vegetables, such as mushrooms, asparagus, or broccoli, quickly turning simple ingredients into a healthful, delicious repast. The crêpes can be made several hours before serving. Simply stack them on a plate and cover with plastic wrap to prevent them from drying out.

FILLING

3 cups Cashew Cream Cheese (page 20)

4½ tablespoons maple syrup

TOPPING

1½ tablespoons canola oil

6 crisp, sweet apples (such as Fuji, Gala, or Honeycrisp), peeled and diced

½ cup maple syrup

1½ teaspoons ground cinnamon

¾ to 1 cup unsweetened apple juice

5. Make the topping.

Heat the oil in a large skillet over medium heat. Add the apples and 2 tablespoons of the maple syrup and cook, stirring frequently, until tender and slightly browned, 4 to 5 minutes. Stir in the remaining 6 tablespoons of maple syrup and the cinnamon and cook for 1 minute to allow the flavors to meld; if the apples stick a bit, that's okay. Pour in ¾ cup of the apple juice and stir to loosen any apples that have stuck to the pan. Stir in more apple juice if you'd like a juicier topping. Cook, stirring frequently, for 1 minute.

6. Sauté the crêpes.

Heat a large nonstick skillet over medium heat. Lightly brush or spray with oil. Put the crêpe parcels in the pan seam-side down and decrease the heat to medium-low. Cook until the bottom is lightly browned, about 4 minutes. Carefully turn over and cook until the other side is lightly browned, about 3 minutes. Serve immediately, topped with the apples.

NOTE: Using the right pan is of the utmost importance. A thin omelet or crêpe pan works best, as it will heat up and cool down quickly. A nonstick 8-inch pan also works well. My favorite is a thin, enameled steel pan; it makes beautiful crêpes. The next most important thing is to be sure to heat the pan adequately before attempting to cook the crêpes.

Even if you don't usually make yeasted breads, give these tender pastries a try. Unlike the traditional dough for Danish pastries, which is loaded with butter and tricky to handle, this version just contains a moderate amount of oil and is therefore easier to work with, even for novices. The key is to keep the dough as soft as possible without being sticky. You can use either maple syrup or brown rice syrup in the dough; maple syrup will yield a sweeter pastry. Here's a bonus: you can also use this dough for cinnamon rolls or other pastries if you like.

cheese DANISHES

MAKES 16 DANISH PASTRIES

DOUGH

2 tablespoons warm water
(110 degrees F)

2¼ teaspoons active dry yeast

1½ teaspoons sugar, evaporated cane juice, or maple syrup

1 cup plain or vanilla soy milk or canned coconut milk

¼ cup raw cashews

¼ cup maple syrup or brown rice syrup

2 tablespoons canola oil

1 teaspoon salt

¾ teaspoon ground cardamom

2½ to 3 cups all-purpose flour, plus more for dusting and kneading

FILLING

1 cup Cashew Cream Cheese (page 20)

¼ cup maple syrup

1½ teaspoons vanilla extract

1. **Mix the dough.**
Put the water in a large bowl and sprinkle the yeast and sugar over the surface. Let sit for about 5 minutes, until bubbly. Mix well. Put the soy milk and cashews in a blender and process until smooth and creamy. Pour into the yeast mixture. Add the maple syrup, oil, salt, and cardamom and mix well. Add 2½ cups of the flour, ½ cup at a time, mixing with a wooden spoon after each addition. Stir in the remaining flour, a few tablespoons at a time, only as needed to make a very soft but not too sticky dough.

2. **Knead the dough.**
To knead by hand, turn the dough out onto a floured work surface and knead until smooth and pliable but still very soft, about 8 minutes, adding flour only as needed to prevent sticking. To knead with an electric mixer with a dough hook, mix until the dough starts to pull away from the sides of the bowl, 6 to 7 minutes. Do not over-knead. Transfer to a clean, lightly oiled bowl, cover with a clean kitchen towel, and let rise in a warm place, until doubled in size, about 1 hour.

3. **Make the filling.**
Put the cream cheese, maple syrup, and vanilla extract in a medium bowl and mix with a wooden spoon until creamy.

Per pastry: calories: 190, protein: 5 g, fat: 7 g, saturated fat: 1 g, carbohydrate: 26 g, sodium: 146 mg, calcium: 16 mg

4. Shape the dough.

Lightly brush or spray 2 baking sheets with oil or line them with parchment paper. When the dough has doubled in bulk, deflate it by punching it down all over with a fist. Turn it out onto a lightly floured work surface and cut it into four equal pieces. Knead one piece a few times, then roll it back and forth to form a log 1 to 1½ inches in diameter. Use a rolling pin to flatten the log from one end to form a long rectangle measuring 16 x 4 inches, and about ¼ inch thick. Cut the rectangle into four 4-inch lengths to form squares. Repeat with the remaining three pieces.

5. Fill the pastries.

Put about 1 rounded tablespoon of the filling in the center of each piece of dough and spread it diagonally from one corner to the opposite corner. Fold in the two other corners, bringing them up to meet in the middle and pressing them together so they adhere. Repeat with the remaining dough and filling, placing the pastries on the prepared baking sheets as you go and spacing them about 2 inches apart.

6. Let the pastries rise.

Cover with clean kitchen towels and let rise in a warm place until almost doubled in size, 30 to 60 minutes.

7. Preheat the oven and bake.

Preheat the oven to 350 degrees F. Bake the pastries for about 20 minutes, until golden brown.

Ricotta adds a light and creamy texture to these tasty pancakes. Dotted with blueberries, they make an exquisite breakfast or brunch entrée.

lemon-scented ricotta PANCAKES WITH BLUEBERRIES

MAKES 8 TO 10 PANCAKES
(4 TO 5 SERVINGS)

1 cup plain or vanilla nondairy milk

2 tablespoons Ener-G egg replacer (see page 134)

1 cup Almond Ricotta (page 47)

2 tablespoons maple syrup, plus more for serving

2 teaspoons vanilla extract

Grated zest of 1 lemon

1 cup whole wheat pastry flour

1 teaspoon baking powder

½ teaspoon salt

1 cup fresh or frozen blueberries

1. **Prepare the batter.**

Put the milk and egg replacer in a blender. Process until frothy and doubled in quantity (this could take as long as 2 minutes). Pour into a large bowl. Add the ricotta, maple syrup, vanilla extract, and lemon zest and mix well. Sift the flour, baking powder, and salt into a medium bowl. Add to the ricotta mixture and stir just until evenly combined. Gently fold in the blueberries.

2. **Cook the pancakes.**

Heat a griddle over medium heat. Lightly brush or spray with oil. Portion the batter onto the hot griddle, using ½ cup of the batter for each pancake. Cook the pancakes on one side until bubbles appear on top, about 3 minutes. Flip and cook the other side until golden brown, about 3 minutes. Serve with maple syrup.

Per serving: calories: 288, protein: 11 g, fat: 10 g, saturated fat: 1 g, carbohydrate: 38 g, sodium: 358 mg, calcium: 146 mg

Glossary

Agar. Known as *kanten* in Japanese and macrobiotic cooking, agar is a sea vegetable with excellent gelling properties. It is sold in a variety of forms, from powder to flakes to bars, and is available online and often at natural food stores. When the recipes in this book offer an option of agar or carrageenan, I call for the powdered form of agar. When only agar is used, I give you the option of using powder or flakes. In any form, agar must be mixed with liquid, simmered, and completely dissolved to activate its gelling properties. Mixtures made with agar will set at room temperature, but chilling it will expedite the process. Once set, the gelled mixtures will be quite firm, rather than wobbly like desserts made with conventional gelatin. When substituting agar powder for carrageenan powder, use twice as much. When substituting agar flakes for agar powder, use three times as much.

Arborio rice. Arborio rice is a pearly, short-grain Italian rice that has a creamy texture when cooked.

Arrowroot starch. Also called arrowroot powder or arrowroot flour, arrowroot starch is made from the root of a tropical plant. It is an excellent thickener for sauces because it has a neutral flavor and, unlike flour, yields a clear final appearance, rather than cloudy.

Carrageenan. A natural carbohydrate derived from Irish moss, carrageenan is widely used in the food industry as a thickening agent. My experience is that, tablespoon for tablespoon, carrageenan powder has about twice the thickening and gelling power of powdered agar. It also produces a slightly more gelatinous, rather than firm, texture. Unlike mixtures made with agar, which don't melt once they have set, those made with carrageenan will return to a liquid state when exposed to heat. Therefore, carrageenan is a better choice for making cheeses that melt. It is available online (see Resources). Be sure to purchase kappa carrageenan, rather than iota, which produces softer gels, or lambda, which doesn't have gelling properties.

There has been some concern about the safety of carrageenan and fear that it might be carcinogenic. I researched this and learned that the ill effects were observed in animal studies that used a non-food-grade form of carrageenan altered by the addition of an acid. Food-grade carrageenan hasn't been shown to be carcinogenic, either in animals or humans.

Cacao nibs. Cacao nibs (sometimes erroneously spelled cocoa nibs) are simply raw cacao beans that have been lightly crushed into bits.

Chipotle chiles in adobo sauce. Chipotle chiles are dried jalapeños. They are available in several forms, including in small cans, packed in flavorful, smoky adobo sauce. You can find canned chipotle chiles in adobo sauce at most grocery stores with the Mexican or Latin American foods.

Coconut milk. Coconut milk is milk made from the meat of the coconut and is not to be confused with coconut water, which is the liquid inside the coconut. While it is possible to make coconut milk at home, it's so much easier to use canned coconut milk, so that's what the recipes in this book call for. Make sure you purchase full-fat, not light, coconut milk.

Coconut sugar. I like to use coconut sugar in recipes that call for larger amounts of sugar. It's akin to brown sugar in flavor but has a much lower glycemic index, so it doesn't spike blood sugar levels. It lends a mild, rather than cloying, sweetness to baked goods.

Ener-G egg replacer. Egg replacer is a powdery combination of various starches and leavening ingredients that is mixed with water and used in place of eggs. Several brands are available, and they vary in how much is used to replace each egg and in the quantity of water used. Because I prefer and recommend Ener-G egg replacer, that's what the recipes in this book call for. It is readily available in natural food stores and from many online retailers.

Miso. Miso is a paste made by fermenting soybeans, sometimes with the addition of other legumes or grains. It imparts both saltiness and an aged, slightly cheeselike taste to the recipes in this book, adding complexity and layers of flavor. There are hundreds of varieties of miso in Japan, and while you won't find as many in the United States, the number of varieties here is increasing. For the purposes of this book, choose one that is light to medium brown or tan in color (not white or dark red). These are often labeled as "light," "mellow," or "mild." Because I find the labeling of miso in the United States to be confusing, I have referred to miso in this book by its color, which is usually an indicator of flavor, including degree of mellowness, saltiness, and sweetness. If the ingredients include rice, the miso tends to be slightly milder and sweeter, which is perfect for the recipes in this book. Don't use a dark red, overly salty miso.

Nutritional yeast flakes. Nutritional yeast is made from deactivated yeast that was grown specifically for nutritional purposes. It is high in calcium, other minerals, and many vitamins including B vitamins and particularly B_{12}, which is often lacking in vegan diets. Nutritional yeast lends a cheeselike flavor and depth to dishes. It is available in both flake and powdered forms, often in the bulk section of natural food stores. The recipes in this book use nutritional yeast flakes, not the powder.

Panko. Panko is also known as panko breadcrumbs, although this is redundant, because "panko" means breadcrumbs in Japanese. These light, dry breadcrumbs, which are increasingly available in grocery stores and natural food stores, yield a light, crispy texture when used as a coating for foods that are fried or baked.

Tapioca flour. Derived from the root of the cassava plant, tapioca flour is a gluten-free, grain-free powder that's an excellent thickening agent. It produces a gooey consistency that's perfect for cheeses. It is widely available in grocery stores and natural food stores.

Tofu. There are many different kinds of tofu. The types I call for in this book are medium-firm, also called medium or regular, and silken tofu. Both come packed in water and are sold refrigerated.

Umeboshi paste. Japanese pickled plums (umeboshi) are used to make this salty, highly fragrant condiment, which is available at most natural food stores.

Xanthan gum. Xanthan gum is a thickening agent that adds a gooey, slightly stretchy feel to some of the cheeses in this book. It is produced by a process that involves fermentation of sugars by the bacteria *Xanthomonas campestris*. It is available at natural food stores and online. Leaving out the xanthan gum in the recipes where it is called for won't affect flavor, just some of the texture. Guar gum can be substituted in most of the recipes. Where possible, I call for using tapioca flour to achieve the same results.

Agar, Carrageenan, and Xanthan Gum

You can almost assuredly find agar and xanthan gum at natural food stores. Carrageenan is harder to come by, but you may find it at well-stocked natural food stores or home-brewing supply shops. Note that carrageenan may be labeled "Irish moss powder." Of course, you can easily order all three online. Here are some websites where they are available:

- **amazon.com.** A good source for agar, carrageenan, xanthan gum, and just about any other nonperishable ingredient you can't find locally.

- **barryfarm.com.** Agar powder and xanthan gum.

- **bulkfoods.com.** Agar, xanthan gum, tapioca flour, arrowroot powder, and many other natural foods in bulk.

- **iherb.com.** Agar powder and xanthan gum.

- **lepicerie.com.** Agar, carrageenan, xanthan gum, and other hard-to-find ingredients, and also high-quality chocolate, flavoring extracts, exotic condiments and spices, and more.

- **modernistpantry.com.** A good source for carrageenan in reasonable quantities.

Nuts and Seeds

Most natural food stores carry a wide selection of nuts and seeds in bulk. Well-stocked supermarkets can also be good sources, especially if they have bulk bins. Whole Foods Market and Trader Joe's both have good selections at reasonable prices. When purchasing raw cashews, keep in mind that cashew pieces are usually more economical and perfectly adequate for any recipe where they are blended, as is always the case with the recipes in this book. Should you need to purchase these ingredients online, here are some good sources:

- **amazon.com.** A wide variety of nuts and seeds, both conventional and organic, at better prices than most online purveyors.

- **bobsredmill.com.** A limited selection of nuts and seeds, along with a wide range of grains, flours, and other natural foods, including xanthan gum and tapioca flour.

- **bulkfoods.com.** Conventionally grown nuts and seeds in bulk.

- **fruitsstar.com.** Offers nuts and seeds, both conventional and organic, in one-pound and often five-pound packages.

Oils and Vinegars

Natural food and specialty stores, such as Whole Foods Market and Trader Joe's are good sources for high-quality oils and vinegars. Regarding coconut oil, note that for most savory dishes or in any situation where you don't want a strong coconut flavor, it's important to use refined coconut oil. Spectrum brand organic refined coconut oil is a good choice. Should you need to purchase these items online, here are some sources:

- **amazon.com.** A wide variety of oils and vinegars, including Spectrum organic refined coconut oil.

- **globalgardensonline.com.** High-quality olive oils and unusual varieties of vinegar.

- **stonehouseoliveoil.com.** Excellent, high-quality olive oils.

- **vitacost.com.** A wide selection of coconut oil, including Spectrum organic refined coconut oil.

- **wildernessfamilynaturals.com.** Offers "organic, ultra-clean, supreme expeller-pressed" coconut oil, which doesn't have a strong coconut flavor.

Index

umeboshi paste, 135

About the Author

Miyoko Schinner has been a vegetarian for more than forty years and vegan for more than half of that time. She is the author of *The New Now and Zen Epicure* and *Japanese Cooking: Contemporary and Traditional*. Miyoko has been teaching, cooking, and writing about vegan foods for more than thirty years and lives in Northern California with her husband, children, dog, cats, and pet chickens.

BookPublishing Co.

books that educate, inspire, and empower

To find your favorite vegetarian and healthy-living books online, visit:
BookPubCo.com

**Japanese Cooking
Contemporary & Traditional**

Miyoko Nishimoto Schinner

978-1-57067-072-5

$14.95

The New Now and Zen Epicure

Miyoko Nishimoto Schinner

978-1-57067-114-2

$19.95

Cooking Vegan

*Vesanto Melina, MS, RD,
and Joseph Forest*

978-1-57067-267-5

$19.95

Teff Love

Kittee Berns

978-1-57067-311-5

$19.95

Vegan for One

*Ellen Jaffe Jones
with Beverly Lynn Bennett*

978-157067-351-1

$17.95

**Anti-Inflammatory
Foods and Recipes**

Beverly Lynn Bennett

978-1-57067-341-2

$17.95

Purchase these health titles and cookbooks from your local bookstore or natural food store,
or you can buy them directly from:

Book Publishing Company • P.O. Box 99 • Summertown, TN 38483 • 1-888-260-8458

Free shipping and handling on all orders.